The New York Times

PUBLIC PROFILES

Martin Luther King Jr.

EDUCATIONAL PUBLISHING
BOOKS

THE NEW YORK TIMES EDITORIAL STAFF

**Published in 2019 by New York Times Educational Publishing
in association with The Rosen Publishing Group, Inc.
29 East 21st Street, New York, NY 10010**

First Edition

Cataloging-in-Publication Data
Names: New York Times Company.
Title: Martin Luther King Jr. / edited by the New York Times editorial staff.
Description: New York : The New York Times Educational Publishing, 2019. | Series: Public profiles | Includes glossary and index.
Identifiers: ISBN 9781642820317 (pbk.) | ISBN 9781642820300 (library bound) | ISBN 9781642820294 (ebook)
Subjects: LCSH: King, Martin Luther, Jr., 1929–1968—Juvenile literature. | African Americans—Civil rights—History—20th century—Juvenile literature. | Civil rights workers—United States—Biography—Juvenile literature.
Classification: LCC E185.97.K5 M378 2019 | DDC 323.092 B—dc23

Manufactured in the United States of America

On the cover: Dr. Martin Luther King Jr. addresses attendees gathered for the Prayer Pilgrimage for Freedom at the Lincoln Memorial in Washington, D.C., on May 17, 1957; George Tames/The New York Times.

Contents

CHAPTER 2

From Protest to Jail and Back

CHAPTER 3

A Conflicted Civil Rights Movement

CHAPTER 5

'Martin Luther King Is Slain in Memphis'

Introduction

MARTIN LUTHER KING JR. had a dream. With this dream, he persuaded a nation to believe in the possibility of peace, harmony and racial equality.

Rev. Dr. Martin Luther King Jr. was a civil rights activist during a time when Jim Crow laws in the deep South segregated blacks from whites, and civil rights were largely theoretical, existing on paper but not particularly in practice. Dr. King believed it was possible to change this and to improve the lives of black people through desegregation and equal voting rights. Inspired by his Christian faith and the success of Mohandas Gandhi's passive resistance in freeing India from Great Britain's rule, Dr. King pursued a relentless path of nonviolent protest through rallies, marches and boycotts. And he inspired hundreds of thousands of people — black and white — to join him.

Dr. King's actions exposed the unfair and brutally oppressive conditions to which black people were subjected every day. He also called attention to the value of blacks in the workforce and the positive role of black people in civil society. Dr. King was revered by the people for whom he advocated and reviled by many in power. Devoted to his people and his cause, he stoically faced repeated harassment, threats, arrests and physical harm. And he prevailed.

Dr. King led the Montgomery Bus Boycott, which resulted in the desegregation of public transportation throughout Alabama and other states. He rallied black people to demand equal voting and housing laws. He campaigned for improved wages, working conditions and schools. He advised parishioners, other civil rights leaders and presidents. He preached — and practiced — love, forgiveness and equality.

Dr. King's work earned him the Nobel Peace Prize and numerous other awards.

DON CRAVENS/THE LIFE IMAGES COLLECTION/GETTY IMAGES

The Rev. Dr. Martin Luther King, director of the Montgomery bus boycott, outlining strategies to his advisors and fellow organizers, Rev. Ralph D. Abernathy, left, and Rosa Parks, center, who was the catalyst for the protest of bus riders.

Despite his message of peace, Dr. King was a controversial figure. Government officials sought to control him. Militant civil rights leaders clashed with him over using more aggressive methods of protest. Many people believed his opposition to the United States' involvement in the Vietnam war distracted him from his civil rights work.

Dr. King was undaunted. Unwavering, he pursued his mission of nonviolent resistance to the policies and practices he believed compromised the lives and rights of black people.

His many accolades and achievements, however, could not protect Dr. King from deep prejudice and fear. On April 4, 1968, after a decade as the civil rights voice of a nation and a people, Dr. King was assassinated by a white man outside his motel in Memphis, Tennessee.

Martin Luther King Jr. is honored as a hero who fought for justice and equality. His cause is still being fought today.

CHAPTER 1

Protest – In the Name of Love

At the age of 27, Rev. Dr. Martin Luther King Jr. had a family, a home and a good job as pastor of a middle-class Baptist church in Montgomery, Ala. He also had a vision. Armed with a deep Christian faith and doctoral degrees in theology and philosophy, Dr. King believed in justice and equality. He believed in improving the lives of all people through compassion, understanding and love. And he was willing to sacrifice everything to make his vision a reality.

Negroes Pledge to Keep Boycott

BY WAYNE PHILLIPS | FEB. 24, 1956

MONTGOMERY, ALA., FEB. 23 — One after the other, indicted Negro leaders took the rostrum in a crowded Baptist church tonight to urge their followers to shun the city's buses and "walk with God."

More than 2,000 Negroes filled the church from basement to balcony and overflowed into the street. They chanted and sang; they shouted and prayed; they collapsed in the aisles and they sweltered in an 85-degree heat. They pledged themselves again and again to "passive resistance."

It is under this banner that they have carried on for eighty days a stubborn boycott of the city's buses. The boycott has brought criminal charges against Negro leaders.

Eighty-nine of them, including twenty-four Protestant ministers, were arrested yesterday and today and charged with carrying on an illegal boycott. More arrests are to be made under eleven indictments handed up Tuesday,

Tomorrow those arrested are to be arraigned in Circuit Court. The Negroes have been called on to stage at that time a "prayer pilgrimage day" — to give up the use of automobiles and taxis and walk the streets in protest.

"It is not expected that a single race-loving Negro will turn the key in his ignition or turn the crank of his automobile or ride a taxicab," the Rev. Ralph D. Abernathy told tonight's meeting. "And we know," he added, "that nobody will ride the buses."

Mr. Abernathy, 29 years old, is the pastor of the First Baptist Church, where the meeting was held. He headed the negotiating committee that tried unsuccessfully to settle the boycott that was organized Dec. 5. The boycott was a protest against the arrest of a Negro woman who refused to give up a seat in the white section of a bus.

"We're not trying to impress anybody with our strength," Mr. Abernathy said. "We just plan to demonstrate to the people who do not have cars that we're willing to walk with them."

Sixty-five per cent of the city's bus passengers before the boycott were Negroes. Since then boycotted buses have plied the streets almost empty, while Negroes make their way to and from work in taxis, with the aid of a 300-car auto pool, or on foot.

As the negroes waited for the meeting to start they sang, picking up the hymns that sprang to mind.

When the leaders appeared at the rear of the church the audience stood and shouted and whistled and waved and cheered. The program opened with, a hymn — "Onward Christian Soldiers" — and a prayer to God "not to leave us in this hour." The scripture was from Corinthians I — "If I have no love I count for nothing." And then they sang "O lift me up and let me stand on higher ground."

Rev. Martin Luther King Jr., head of the Montgomery Improvement Association, which has directed the eighty-day boycott, told the gathering that the protest was not against a single incident but over things that "go deep down into the archives of history."

"We have known humiliation, we have known abusive language, we have been plunged into the abyss of oppression," he told them. "And we decided to rise up only with the weapon of protest. It is one of the greatest glories of America that we have the right of protest."

"There are those who would try to make of this a hate campaign," the Atlanta-born, Boston-educated Baptist minister said. "This is not war between the white and the Negro but a conflict between justice and injustice. This is bigger than the Negro race revolting against the white. We are seeking to improve not the Negro of Montgomery but the whole of Montgomery.

"If we are arrested every day, if we are exploited every day, if we are trampled over every day, don't ever let anyone pull you so low as to hate them. We must use the weapon of love. We must have compassion and understanding for those who hate us. We must realize so many people are taught to hate us that they are not totally responsible for their hate. But we stand in life at midnight, we are always on the threshold of a new dawn."

His talk was followed by a prayer by the Rev. S. S. Seay, former executive secretary of the African Methodist Episcopal Zion Church – "A prayer for those who oppose us."

The Rev. A. W. Wilson, vice president of the Negro Alabama Baptist convention, brought greetings to the meeting from Negro Baptists throughout the state. "No other race but the Negro race," he said, "could smile as we have smiled tonight, and sing as we sang tonight and get happy and shout as we have shouted tonight."

Battle Against Tradition: Martin Luther King Jr.

BY THE NEW YORK TIMES | MARCH 21, 1956

MONTGOMERY, ALA., MARCH 20 — The battle against segregation in Montgomery is being led by young, southern-born but often northern-educated Negroes. For some of them it has meant a break with the views of their parents; for all of them it has meant taking a strong stand against the traditions of their community. But in their current efforts, they have solidly behind them the counsel and support of their elders.

Outstanding among these young leaders, whose ages range from 25 to 32, is the Rev. Dr. Martin Luther King Jr. He is president of the Montgomery Improvement Association, which was organized to lead the current protest against bus segregation. Dr. King is the first to be tried of ninety-three persons arrested in connection with the boycott of Montgomery buses by Negroes.

Dr. King is a rather soft-spoken man with a learning and maturity far beyond his twenty-seven years. His clothes are in conservative good taste and he has a small trim mustache.

He heads an upper middle-class group of Negro Baptists with dignity and restraint.

They worship in the historic Dexter Avenue Baptist Church. This is a red-brick building on the edge of the State Capitol Mall, near the long white marble steps atop which Jefferson Davis took his oath as President of the Confederacy.

Dr. King came here as pastor of the church in September 1954, after finishing work on his Doctor of Philosophy degree at Boston University. He is particularly well read in Kant and Hegel, and the concepts of struggle as a law of growth.

Dr. King is a Baptist preacher in a great southern tradition of resounding, repetitive rhetoric. And he can build to his climax with a crescendo of impassioned pulpit-pounding that overwhelms the listener with the depth of his convictions.

Among his convictions are these: That all men are basically good; that ultimately good will triumph over the evil in their nature; that segregation in all its aspects is evil, and that ultimately it must be swept away.

He continues to teach this doctrine in public in the heart of a state officially committed to defend segregation at all cost.

"Frankly, I am for immediate integration," he said. "Segregation is evil and as a minister I cannot condone evil."

He sees the current bus boycott as just one aspect of a world-wide revolt of oppressed peoples.

Dr. King's maternal grandfather was the pastor of the Ebenezer Baptist Church at Atlanta, from 1895 to 1932. His father has been the pastor of the church from 1932 to the present.

Dr. King was his father's assistant at that church from 1948, after receiving his Doctor of Divinity degree, until 1953, when he went to Boston to work on his doctorate.

He did his undergraduate work at Morehouse College, and had his religious training at the Crozier Theological Seminary in Chester, Pa., where he was the top man in his class. He and his wife, a graduate of Antioch College in Ohio, have an 11-week-old daughter.

Another of the young Negro leaders here is the Rev. Ralph D. Abernathy, who is 29. He is pastor of the Negro First Baptist Church, and head of the negotiating committee that tried unsuccessfully last week to settle the boycott.

The only two Negro lawyers in Montgomery also have been leaders in the movement. They are Charles D. Langford, 32, and Fred D. Gray, 25. They have filed a suit to overthrow the city and state segregation laws and are defending the Negroes arrested in connection with the bus protest.

Negro Minister Convicted of Directing Bus Boycott

BY WAYNE PHILLIPS | MARCH 23, 1956

MONTGOMERY, ALA., MARCH 22 — The Rev. Dr. Martin Luther King Jr. was found guilty today of leading an illegal boycott against the Montgomery city bus lines. Circuit Judge Eugene W. Carter fined the 27-year-old Negro Baptist minister $500 and $500 court costs.

The fine and costs were converted into a jail sentence of 386 days because Dr. King chose to appeal rather than to pay the money. However, the sentence was suspended after the defense lawyers served notice of appeal.

Dr. King was released on $1,000 bond. The cases of eighty-nine other Negroes arrested in connection with the protest against the bus lines were continued pending appeal.

The protest began Dec. 5 over the arrest of Mrs. Rosa Parks, a 43-year-old seamstress, for refusing to give up her seat to a white person.

Nearly all of Montgomery's 50,000 Negroes have refused to ride the city buses since then. They have used a pool of 300 automobiles organized by the Montgomery Improvement Association, which is headed by Dr. King.

The protest movement went on without interruption or incident today. There was every indication it would continue to do so until some agreement was reached with the city and the bus company.

Arthur D. Shores, one of the eight lawyers who defended Dr. King in the four-day misdemeanor trial, estimated that it would take three years for the case to come up in the Alabama Court of Appeals.

There was every indication that the case would go from there through the Alabama Supreme Court to the United States Supreme Court on the ground that the conviction violated the constitutional rights of Dr. King under the state and Federal constitutions.

The conviction was under a 1921 statute forbidding the hindering of a lawful business without "just cause or legal excuse."

There was no sign of emotion from the predominantly Negro audience as Judge Carter delivered his finding at 3:56 P. M. as soon as arguments were completed.

Judge Carter announced that he was finding Dr. King guilty, but would fine him only half the possible penalty because he had continually urged his followers to observe a policy of nonviolence.

PREPARED FOR THE 'WORST'

"I was optimistic enough to hope for the best but realistic enough to prepare for the worst," Dr. King told those who gathered around him a few minutes after the verdict.

"This will not mar or diminish in any way my interest in the protest," the young minister said. "We will continue to protest in the same spirit of nonviolence and passive resistance, using the weapon of love."

When Dr. King emerged with his wife at 4:39 P. M., there was a crowd of about 300 Negroes outside the courthouse.

As he appeared, the crowd applauded and shouts went up "Behold the king," and "Long live the king." The Rev. Ralph D. Abernathy, one of the other defendants, called to the crowd: "Don't forget the mass prayer meeting tonight."

"You gonna be there?" a Negro in the crowd shouted, and the gathering chorused back, "Yes."

"You gonna ride the buses?" the same Negro cried, and the crowd roared back, "No!"

Dr. King spoke at the prayer meeting, which was held in the Holt Street Baptist Church. This was the scene of the mass meeting at which it was decided to extend a spontaneous one-day boycott until the bus company bettered conditions.

"This conviction and all the convictions they can heap on me will not diminish my determination one iota," Dr. King said. "God is using Montgomery as his proving ground, and maybe here in the cradle of the Confederacy the idea of freedom in the south and will be born."

The 2,000 Negroes who crowded the church and overflowed onto the street outside whooped and shouted and clapped at his declaration that "the protest is still going on."

Dr. King's lawyers presented nine witnesses this morning in a parade of thirty-four who told of verbal abuse, discourtesy, threats, shooting and other mistreatment at the hands of drivers for the bus company.

Circuit Solicitor William F. Thetford presented six bus drivers as rebuttal witnesses. All testified that they were courteous to Negro passengers.

Judge Carter, who has been on the bench for twenty-one years, teaches the men's monthly Bible class at the Dexter Avenue Methodist Church, almost across the street from Dr. King's church.

The judge is a member of the official board of the church, and as such concurred in a recent decision by the board that Negroes who came there should be asked to worship in their colored churches.

In World War I he served as a first lieutenant in the infantry. He is a Mason, a Shriner and a member of the American Legion.

2,500 Here Hail Boycott Leader

BY STANLEY ROWLAND JR. | MARCH 26, 1956

THE CONVICTED LEADER of the Negro boycott of buses in Montgomery, Ala., was given a hero's welcome by an interracial audience of 2,500 in a Brooklyn church yesterday.

The Rev. Dr. Martin Luther King Jr. preached the doctrine of passive resistance and love as a way for Negroes all over the country to win civil rights.

The audience laughed and wept, cheered and prayed. A collection for the Montgomery protest was taken up in waste baskets, cake boxes, cartons, cooking utensils and other containers. Estimates of the total were in the thousands of dollars.

Outside the Concord Baptist Church at Marcy and Putnam Avenues, two men were trying to sell a Trotskyite newspaper, The Militant, and trying to engage people in conversation. They got no place. One observer remarked that they would have made more money peddling scorpions.

The audience, largely Negro but with a goodly scattering of whites, packed the basement auditorium. Old men sat on the floor. Boys perched in every available corner.

Dr. King told the crowd that the protest would continue in Montgomery "no matter what." He repeatedly emphasized that "love will be returned for hate, nonviolence will be returned for violence. This isn't just a fight for Negroes, it is a fight for justice and democracy."

The invocation was given by the Rev. Archibald V. McLees of Holy Rosary Roman Catholic Church in Brooklyn. Rabbi Eugene J. Sack of Beth Elohim Congregation of Brooklyn also participated in the ceremonies.

Father McLees praised Dr. King and the 50,000 Negroes of Montgomery "for what you are doing and more especially for the Christian spirit in which you are doing it."

Dr. King stressed the Christian basis of the protest. Quoting Christ, "I come not to bring peace but a sword," he declared that the sword was one of nonviolent revolt against "narrow and oppressive traditions."

There was not a single note of bitterness in his talk. There were flashes of wit:

"The South has a heart, but it just has a little heart trouble now."

On Montgomery buses, he said, Negroes were forced to stand while empty seats remained reserved for whites, and pregnant women were told to "go to the rear and stand with the rest of the black apes."

But in spite of this, he declared, "we will not resort to violence, we will not degrade ourselves with hatred.

"We will return good for evil, we will love our enemies — not the way you love your wife, but the mighty, transcendent God-given love for our brother men, white and dark. Christ showed us the way and Gandhi in India showed it could work."

The Rev. Gardner Taylor, pastor of the church, appealed for funds for the Montgomery protest.

Checks for $100 and more came first. Then came ten and twenty dollar bills. A wisp of a white girl — blonde, about 11 years old shyly dumped the contents of her piggy-bank into a collection basket. An old woman cupped her hands to cover a sneeze and someone dropped a five-dollar bill in them. She ran with it to the nearest collection container — a shoe box — and then sneezed.

Dr. King, who was fined $500 plus $500 in costs for conducting the boycott, said he would appeal his conviction to the Supreme Court, if necessary.

After the meeting, Dr. King departed for Montgomery. The crowd flowed out into the crisp Palm Sunday evening. Someone was still hawking the Trotskyite paper. Nobody was buying.

Bus Integration in Alabama Calm

BY GEORGE BARRETT | DEC. 22, 1956

MONTGOMERY, ALA., DEC. 21 — The Negroes of Montgomery, victors in a year-long boycott to end segregation in public transit here, quietly and in determined numbers went back on the city's desegregated buses today.

For the first time in this "cradle of the Confederacy" all the Negroes entered buses through the front door. They sat in the first empty seats they saw, in the front of buses and in the rear. They did not get up to give a white passenger a seat. And whites sat with Negroes.

As one of the oldest race barriers in this deep South community fell this morning, following a formal order from the Supreme Court to abolish segregation in local buses, nothing happened to indicate that Montgomery's 75,000 whites and 50,000 Negroes looked upon the historic event as anything but a natural development.

There were no special details of police on duty, nor were they needed. Despite alarms by city officials and members of the White Citizens Council during the last year that bus desegregation in Montgomery would bring riots and bloodshed, only one minor incident marred today's changeover from long established custom.

A Negro woman who was one of the first to board the newly desegregated buses this morning was slapped in the face by a white youth as she stepped out of a bus into the street. She reported that her assailant then jumped into a car with an out-of-state license plate and sped away with a group of white men.

In a couple of instances, carloads of white men were seen to follow some of the buses, but no overt attempt was made to interfere with the bus company's decision to carry out the Supreme Court order.

Aboard the buses as the Negroes and the whites for the first time sat where they both chose to sit, the talk was rarely about integration. At first there was no exchange between whites and Negroes as they took up the strange pattern of mixed seating. But often the stiffness gradually disappeared.

A Negro turned in one bus to ask a white passenger sitting behind him — the mark of the new order — what time it was and got a quick courteous reply. A white man who had been sitting next to a Negro, said later he did not understand what all the fuss and the difficulty had been about.

The Rev. Dr. Martin Luther King Jr., the 27-year-old Negro minister who was a leader in the boycott, rode one of the city buses today — accompanied by a white minister, the Rev. Glenn Smiley.

MINISTER OPTIMISTIC

While there was still fear in the community that efforts might be made to disrupt the bus integration process, Dr. King stressed the harmony that had marked the crucial first day of desegregation and predicted no major trouble in the future.

"If any trouble does occur I feel the proper authorities will take cognizance and that it will be stopped immediately," he added.

In some cases white passengers made sneering remarks, but Dr. King's emphasis on the Christian theme of love between all men has been adopted by the Negro community not only as a tenet, but as a tactic in their struggle for racial equality.

Two white men in one bus today found themselves sitting behind a Negro, and one of the whites said, loudly: "I see this isn't going to be a white Christmas."

The Negro looked up, and smiled. He said, with good humor but firmness: "Yes, sir, that's right." Everybody in the bus smiled, and all rancor seemed to evaporate.

There was no mass turnout of Negroes today to exploit their victory. For the most part, only those who had planned already to go to town took the buses. They made nothing special of it, simply abandoned their yearlong custom of walking, or joining in a car pool, and quietly boarded the bus.

© AP IMAGES/HAROLD VALENTINE

Negroes in Montgomery were free to sit where they chose. Among the first riders were Rev. Ralph D. Abernathy, left, and the Rev. Martin Luther King Jr., who had been active in the boycott of buses.

There had been speculation that the whites might start their own bus boycott now, rather than ride with Negroes. Yet many whites were among today's passengers.

The Negroes, under Dr. King, held almost 100 per cent to their campaign, and consequent losses to the midtown area had brought quiet pressures from merchants and many other responsible groups in Montgomery to end the fight.

Shot Hits Home of Bus Bias Foe

BY GEORGE BARRETT | DEC. 24, 1956

MONTGOMERY, ALA., DEC. 23 — A shotgun blast was fired early this morning into the home of the Negro minister who led the successful fight to abolish racial segregation on Montgomery's buses.

The Rev. Martin Luther King Jr. said that he and his family had been asleep when the shotgun pellets pierced the front door at about 1:30 this morning.

The Kings live in a small bungalow in an upper middle-class Negro section. The house was the target of a bomb several months ago.

This morning panes of glass were shattered, but the damage was slight and no one was hurt. Mrs. King said that she had looked out over the front lawn, where floodlights have been shining since the integration fight started here a little over a year ago, and had seen a taxi turning around at the corner.

Dr. King, whose policy of nonviolence has set the pattern for the Negro community in the struggle for bus segregation, made no report to the police.

His disclosure of the shooting was in keeping with his campaign for understanding and love between Montgomery's whites and Negroes and with his pleas to the community's 50,000 Negroes always to turn the other cheek.

NEW STRUGGLE PLANNED

Meantime, at a rally held tonight at one of the Negro churches to commemorate the victory in the bus battle, Dr. King told several hundred persons that the fight for racial integration would be extended to the public schools and recreation areas here.

"We cannot rest in Montgomery until every public school is integrated," Dr. King told a quietly jubilant audience.

MICHAEL OCHS ARCHIVES/GETTY IMAGES

The Rev. Dr. Martin Luther King in a relaxed moment at home in May with his wife, Coretta King, and daughter, Yolanda.

He predicted that some of the white people who had supported the battle to integrate the buses would turn against the Negroes on the school fight. But he stressed that the Negroes had to wage battle for the principles upheld by the Supreme Court.

At his regular Sunday morning service at the red brick Dexter Avenue Baptist Church, Dr. King softly and without emotion told his congregation about the shooting.

He included the shooting announcement among others about the need for Christmas baskets for the poor — both white and Negro — and the plea to make sure that those who were sick would not go unvisited.

He told his congregation that he would have liked to meet those who had done the shooting to tell them that surely they must know they could not solve problems that way. Still without raising his voice, he said he would have liked to point out that even if he were killed his attackers would have 50,000 other Negroes here to "get."

Dr. King went on to say that as the walls of segregation continued to crumble in the South "it may be that some of us may have to die." But he called on his congregation never to falter, never to forget that in the midst of changes in life, of changes in man, even "if the stars no longer bedeck the heavens," God's love for all things and for all men would continue.

There was no stir in the congregation, no sign that anyone was surprised.

They and virtually all the other Negroes in Montgomery have subscribed to Dr. King's rule to practice Christian love in their everyday conduct. After their pastor's announcement of the attack, the congregation calmly picked up the hymnals and sang "Silent Night, Holy Night."

Montgomery's Negroes have been riding on desegregated buses for three days without a major incident. Dr. King suggested that there was a higher law than the South's insistence that the Negro "keep his place."

"The glory to God that puts man in his place will make brothers of us all," Dr. King declared.

In Birmingham, Negroes have announced their resolve to sit where they choose in that city's buses.

The Rev. E. L. Shuttlesworth, pastor of the Bethel Baptist Church there and head of the Alabama Christian Movement for Human Rights, said that "some" Negroes probably would sit in seats reserved for whites starting Thursday.

The Negroes have served notice on the City Council there that they intend to challenge segregation.

The expectation is that the Council, which meets on Wednesday, will contend that Birmingham is not affected by the Supreme Court ruling.

Mr. Shuttlesworth predicted that the first Negro who attempted to sit in the front of a bus would be arrested. He said that after the arrest their legal battle to desegregate Birmingham's buses would begin.

Negroes Hold Rally On Rights in Capital

BY JAY WALZ | MAY 18, 1957

WASHINGTON, MAY 17 — Thousands of civil rights advocates met at the Lincoln Memorial today in a three-hour demonstration. The rally was sponsored by Negro organizations.

The Prayer Pilgrimage for Freedom, which drew large numbers of Negroes from thirty states, observed the third anniversary of the Supreme Court decision outlawing segregation in public schools.

The pitch and pace of the ceremony rose as Negro leaders called on President Eisenhower to "speak out more firmly" for civil rights, and on Congress to act.

The Rev. Martin Luther King Jr. of Montgomery, Ala., told the assembly that the judicial branch of the Government had shown "strong, aggressive leadership" on civil rights issues.

As the crowd shouted loud "amens" in approval, the 28-year-old preacher asserted that the executive branch was "all too silent and apathetic," and the legislative branch "too stagnant and hypocritical."

Representative Adam Clayton Powell Jr., Democrat of Manhattan, called for an American third force to fight for civil rights.

"We meet here in front of the Lincoln Memorial," he said, "because we are getting more from a dead Republican than we are getting from live Democrats and live Republicans."

The assembly, which gathered under cloudy skies, overflowed the memorial steps, spread over Memorial Circle and occupied the greensward, around the end of the reflecting pool. A few white persons attended the rally. Melvin Leach, Park Police inspector, estimated the crowd at 15,000. But pilgrimage leaders said this figure was much too low. The Rev. Thomas Kilgore Jr., pastor of Friendship Baptist Church in New York, who was national director of the pilgrimage, said at least 27,000 persons were present.

GEORGE TAMES/THE NEW YORK TIMES

Rev. Dr. Martin Luther King Jr. speaking at the Prayer Pilgrimage for Freedom at the Lincoln Memorial in Washington, D.C.

THRONG CALLED ORDERLY

The metropolitan police, anticipating a traffic jam, had canceled all leaves for the day. But afterward the police said the crowd had moved in and out of the memorial area in a most orderly way.

Prayers, musical selections and scripture readings interlarded the speaking program, and the printed program asked that applause be withheld because of the religious nature of the ceremony.

However, A. Philip Randolph, a co-chairman of the rally, relaxed this request as the program got under way by suggesting that listeners might show approval by waving handkerchiefs and saying "Amens."

They did.

Mr. Randolph, who is president of the Brotherhood of Sleeping Car Porters, had been applauded when in opening remarks he warned against the acceptance of Communist help.

"We know that Communists have no genuine interest in the solution of problems of racial discrimination," Mr. Randolph said, "but seek only to use this issue to strengthen the foreign policy of the Soviet Union."

Mr. Randolph praised President Eisenhower for his "high sense of humanity," but called on him to "speak out" against the "lawlessness, terror and fears that hang like a pall over the hearts of citizens of color in the South."

The House Rules Committee, which has had the civil rights bill under parliamentary consideration for several weeks, ended hearings today. It plans to vote Tuesday on reporting the bill out for floor action.

In the Senate, the Judiciary Committee is considering amendments attached to its civil rights bill by Southern Senators.

Roy Wilkins, executive secretary of the National Association for the Advancement of Colored People, said Senator James O. Eastland of Mississippi had "buried" the civil rights bill since February. Mr. Eastland, a Democrat, is chairman of the Judiciary Committee.

Mr. King, who led the Negro boycott on buses in Montgomery in a fight to end segregation on public conveyances, appeared a hero to the pilgrims. He received the biggest ovation of the afternoon when he declared both major political parties had "betrayed the cause of justice."

Mr. King said the Supreme Court ruling three years ago had come as "a joyous daybreak to end the long night of enforced segregation.

"It came as a reaffirmation of the good old American doctrine of freedom and equality for all people," he said.

Negro Leaders Confer With President and Rogers at White House

BY JOSEPH A. LOFTUS | JUNE 24, 1958

WASHINGTON, JUNE 23 — Four Negro leaders asked President Eisenhower today to establish "a clear national policy" against race discrimination and a program to make it effective. The Little Rock setback to school integration, they said, "has shocked and outraged Negro citizens and millions of their fellow Americans." The four said afterward that they believed the President was sympathetic to their cause, but that neither he nor Attorney General William P. Rogers, who also was present, had given them a commitment or a promise of any kind. The Negro leaders have been trying for about a year to see the President. The latest request was made about three weeks ago. The appointment was set before United States District Judge Harry J. Lemley had granted a delay in school integration in Little Rock, Ark., until 1961.

The White House visitors were A. Phillip Randolph, a vice president of the American Federation of Labor and Congress of Industrial Organizations and president of the Brotherhood of Sleeping Car Porters; Lester B. Granger, executive secretary of the National Urban League; the Rev. Dr. Martin Luther King Jr. of Montgomery, Ala., president of the Southern Leadership Conference and leader of the Montgomery bus boycott, and Roy Wilkins, executive secretary of the National Association for the Advancement of Colored People.

The Negro group said that neither the President nor the Attorney General had commented on the Little Rock decision except that Mr. Rogers pointed out that the Justice Department had already announced it had the decision under consideration.

After the meeting with the President, the visitors learned of Judge Lemley's refusal to suspend his order pending an appeal.

ABBIE ROWE/PHOTOQUEST/GETTY IMAGES

Negro leaders with the President and Attorney General William P. Rogers, third from right, at the White House. They are Rev. Dr. Martin Luther King Jr., left, A. Phillip Randolph, center, and Roy Wilkins, right.

Their statement proposed a program of nine points, which they read to the President. They said he did not comment on it but insisted they found him gracious and believed that "our cause has been advanced."

Mr. Wilkins said, "We tried to impress on him that the colored people are frustrated and angry."

These were the main points in the Negroes' program:

• The President should declare that the law will be vigorously upheld with the total resources at his command.

• The President should convoke a White House conference of constructive leadership to discuss ways and means of complying peaceably with the court's rulings.

• Information, resources and advice of the appropriate Government agencies should be made available to all officials and community groups seeking to work out a program of education and action.

• The President should request both political parties to lay aside partisanship and enact a law in order that constitutional rights other than voting rights may be enforced by the Attorney General.

• The President should direct the Department of Justice to give all legal assistance possible in the appeal from the Lemley decision.

• The President should direct the Justice Department to act now to protect the right of citizens to register and vote.

• The President should direct the Justice Department to act against the wave of bombing of churches, synagogues, homes and community centers and the brutality directed against Negroes in Dawson, Ga., and other communities.

• The President should recommend extension of the life of the new Civil Rights Commission for at least a full year beyond its present expiration date.

• The president should make clear that he believes in the principle that Federal money should not be used to underwrite segregation in violation of the constitutional rights of millions of Negro citizens; that this principle should be applied whether in matters of Federal aid to education, hospitals, housing, or any other grants-in-aid to state and local governments.

"These recommendations," the group concluded, "are made in the belief that tensions between citizens in our country, and the anxieties of citizens themselves, will be eased and eventually erased if a clear national policy and a program of implementation are established by the Chief Executive of the nation."

Dr. King, Negro Leader, Stabbed By Woman in a Store in Harlem

BY THE NEW YORK TIMES | SEPT. 21, 1958

THE REV. DR. MARTIN LUTHER KING JR., who organized the Negro bus boycott in Montgomery, Ala., in 1956, was stabbed by a Negro woman in a Harlem department store yesterday.

Dr. King was taken to Harlem Hospital where his condition was described as good. He was stabbed in the upper left side of his chest with a steel letter opener.

At 6:30 P. M. he underwent an operation to remove the letter opener. The operation lasted two-and-a-quarter hours and was performed by Dr. Aubré de L. Maynard, chief of surgery at the hospital.

Dr. Maynard said the operation was a success and "there is every indication that Dr. King will be all right." He said Dr. King would remain at the hospital about two weeks.

His attacker was arrested at the store L. M. Blumstein, Inc., at 230 West 125th Street. She was identified as Mrs. Izola Ware Curry, 42 years old, of 121 West 122d Street.

Governor Harriman went to the hospital from his East Side home. He was joined by a number of Negro leaders.

Mr. Harriman said that Police Commissioner Stephen P. Kennedy had told him Mrs. Curry appeared to be "deranged" and that she was making many "incoherent" statements.

The stabbing occurred at 3:30 P. M. on the ground floor of the department store, which is between Seventh and Eighth Avenues.

Dr. King was seated at a desk in a roped-off rear area autographing copies of his book, "Stride Toward Freedom: The Montgomery Story." The book was published last week.

Several persons were seated near Dr. King at the time of the stabbing, including Arthur B. Spingarn, president of the National Association for the Advancement of Colored People, and Mrs. Anne Hedgman, a member of Mayor Wagner's staff. An honor guard of girl students from Wadleigh Junior High School stood at either side of the desk. Twenty persons were waiting in line to get books autographed.

The police said Mrs. Curry, who was not in the line, stepped through a narrow opening leading to the desk, leaned over and asked, "Are you Mr. King?"

Dr. King nodded. Mrs. Curry, the police said, then pulled the letter opener from her bag and stabbed Dr. King.

She was quoted as saying: "I've been after you for six years. I'm glad I've done it." Detectives said she also made derogatory remarks about the N.A.A.C.P.

Walter Pettiford, an advertising representative of The Amsterdam News, a Negro newspaper, grabbed Mrs. Curry, pinning her arms to her side.

The store's chief security officer, Clifford Jackson, and Harry Dixon, a store guard, who were also in the area, ran over and Mr. Jackson handcuffed Mrs. Curry. She did not resist.

Soon the ambulance from Harlem Hospital arrived. Dr. King, still seated in the chair, was carried into the ambulance. News of the stabbing spread quickly through the neighborhood and attracted 1,500 persons to 125th Street, one of Harlem's main thoroughfares.

Forty persons went to the hospital to offer blood.

Others at the hospital, besides Governor Harriman, were Roy Wilkins, executive secretary of the N.A.A.C.P.; A. Philip Randolph, president of the Brotherhood of Sleeping Car Porters; Hulan Jack, Manhattan Borough President; and Robert Mangum, Deputy Hospitals Commissioner.

Dr. Maynard said the blade of the letter opener, seven inches long, had "impinged on the aorta, a blood vessel near the heart." He said a puncture of the aorta would have caused "instant death."

Detectives said a fully loaded .25-calibre Italian automatic was found inside Mrs. Curry's dress. She said she had purchased the automatic last year in Daytona Beach, Fla., while she was working there as a domestic.

Mrs. Curry was taken to the hospital by police where she was identified by Dr. King. She was then booked on charges of felonious assault and violation of the Sullivan Law. She was to be arraigned this morning in Felony Court.

Inspector John Sexton, in charge of Manhattan East detectives, quoted Mrs. Curry as saying she did not know Dr. King was in the store when she went there.

He said she suffered from a "persecution complex." Mrs. Curry, according to the inspector, said she stabbed Dr. King because then "he would listen to my problems because I've been followed in buses and people have been making me lose my job."

Dr. King arrived here several days ago for lectures and to promote his book. He had planned to return to Alabama at 5:15 P. M. yesterday.

Dr. King, Mr. Harriman and Nelson A. Rockefeller, Republican candidate for Governor, were among the speakers Friday night at an outdoor Harlem rally at 125th Street and Seventh Avenue.

Mr. Rockefeller, in Albany for a campaign appearance, said there last night:

"I was shocked to learn of this tragic occurrence. I fervently hope that his injury will not prove serious and that he soon will be able to resume the important work he has been doing."

The Montgomery bus dispute won prominence because of a 385-day boycott in which most of that city's 50,000 Negroes, under Dr. King's leadership, refused to ride under the traditional separate seating arrangements.

The boycott ended Dec. 21, 1956, when the United States Supreme Court ruled that the city's transport segregation ordinances were unconstitutional. Dr. King is 29 years old. He is married and has a daughter.

He is a soft-spoken scholar of Hegel and Kant, a Doctor of Philosophy and a Doctor of Divinity. He is pastor of the Dexter Avenue Baptist Church in Montgomery and president of the Montgomery Improvement Association, organized to lead the boycott.

Dr. King Stricken with Pneumonia

BY THE NEW YORK TIMES | SEPT. 23, 1958

THE CONDITION OF THE Rev. Dr. Martin Luther King Jr. took a sudden turn for the worse yesterday when he developed pneumonia.

The Negro anti-segregation leader from Montgomery, Ala., has been a patient at Harlem Hospital since Saturday afternoon, when he was stabbed with a steel letter opener by a Negro woman in a Harlem department store.

X-rays taken of Dr. King during the afternoon disclosed the pneumonia. It is lodged in the lower right lung.

Dr. Robert H. Wylie, a thoracic surgery specialist, was summoned and went into consultation with the hospital staff. Dr. Wylie is director of chest service at the Columbia University medical section in Bellevue Hospital.

Asked for an opinion on the condition of the 29-year-old minister, Dr. Bernard B. Nadell, superintendent of the hospital, replied, "Prognosis is guarded." He said Dr. King was running a moderate, fluctuating temperature.

"A complication of pneumonia has developed in the right lower lung, which would be expected post-operatively in this type of case," he said.

An operation for removal of the letter opener was performed Saturday night by a team of surgeons headed by Dr. Aubré de L. Maynard, director of surgery at Harlem Hospital. The weapon had been embedded in the chest near the aorta, the main artery.

CITES KING'S COURAGE

"We are giving Dr. King every protection and consultation possible," Dr. Maynard said last night. "Everything is being done for him."

News of the change in Dr. King's condition brought Governor Harriman to the hospital. He had spent four hours there Saturday night and had not left until assured that the minister was progressing satisfactorily.

Mr. Harriman spent a few minutes last night at Dr. King's bedside, in company with Mrs. Coretta King, the minister's wife. He described Dr. King as a man of "tremendous courage."

The Governor said Dr. Maynard had told him that, despite the pneumonia, Dr. King's general condition was "excellent."

The minister has been on the critical list since his admission.

Mrs. Izola Ware Curry, the 42-year-old woman who stabbed Dr. King, was committed to Bellevue Hospital for mental observation Sunday. Physicians said she was incoherent in giving reasons for her attack.

Dr. King attained national prominence two years ago when he led a 385-day boycott by most of Montgomery's 50,000 Negroes against the city's buses, refusing to ride under separate seating arrangements.

Dr. King was reported to have said that he felt no bitterness toward the woman who stabbed him.

Negro Sitdowns Stir Fear Of Wider Unrest in South

BY CLAUDE SITTON | FEB. 15, 1960

CHARLOTTE, N. C., FEB. 14 — Negro student demonstrations against segregated eating facilities have raised grave questions in the South over the future of the region's race relations. A sounding of opinion in the affected areas showed that much more might be involved than the matter of the Negro's right to sit at a lunch counter for a coffee break.

The demonstrations were generally dismissed at first as another college fad of the "panty-raid" variety. This opinion lost adherents, however, as the movement spread from North Carolina to Virginia, Florida, South Carolina and Tennessee and involved fifteen cities.

Some whites wrote off the episodes as the work of "outside agitators." But even they conceded that the seeds of dissent had fallen in fertile soil.

BACKED BY NEGRO LEADERS

Appeals from white leaders to leaders in the Negro community to halt the demonstrations bore little fruit. Instead of the hoped-for statements of disapproval, many Negro professionals expressed support for the demonstrators.

A handful of white students joined the protests. And several state organizations endorsed it. Among them were the North Carolina Council on Human Relations, an inter-racial group, and the Unitarian Fellowship for Social Justice, which currently has an all-white membership.

Students of race relations in the area contended that the movement reflected growing dissatisfaction over the slow pace of desegregation in schools and other public facilities.

It demonstrated, they said, a determination to wipe out the last vestiges of segregation.

Moreover, these persons saw a shift of leadership to younger, more militant Negroes. This, they said, is likely to bring increasing use of passive resistance. The technique was conceived by Mohandas K. Gandhi of India and popularized among Southern Negroes by the Rev. Dr. Martin Luther King Jr. He led the bus boycott in Montgomery, Ala. He now heads the Southern Christian Leadership Conference, a Negro minister's group, which seeks to end discrimination.

WIDE SUPPORT INDICATED

Negro leaders said that this assessment was correct. They disputed the argument heard among some whites that there was no broad support for the demonstrations outside such organizations as the National Association for the Advancement of Colored People.

There was general agreement on all sides that a sustained attempt to achieve desegregation now, particularly in the Deep South, might breed racial conflict that the region's expanding economy could ill afford.

The spark that touched off the protests was provided by four freshmen at North Carolina Agricultural and Technical College in Greensboro. Even Negroes class Greensboro as one of the most progressive cities in the South in terms of race relations.

On Sunday night, Jan. 31, one of the students sat thinking about discrimination.

"Segregation makes me feel that I'm unwanted," McNeil A. Joseph said later in an interview. "I don't want my children exposed to it."

The 17-year-old student from Wilmington, N. C., said that he approached three of his classmates the next morning and found them enthusiastic over a proposal that they demand service at the lunch counter of a downtown variety store.

About 4:45 P. M. they entered the F. W. Woolworth Company store on North Elm Street in the heart of Greensboro. Mr. Joseph said he bought a tube of toothpaste and the others made similar purchases. Then they sat down at the lunch counter.

REBUKED BY A NEGRO

A Negro woman kitchen helper walked up, according to the students, and told them, "You know you're not supposed to be in here." She later called them "ignorant" and a "disgrace" to their race.

The students then asked a white waitress for coffee.

"I'm sorry but we don't serve colored here," they quote her.

"I beg your pardon," said Franklin McCain, 18, of Washington, "you just served me at a counter two feet away. Why is it that you serve me at one counter and deny me at another. Why not stop serving me at all counters."

The four students sat, coffee-less, until the store closed at 5:30 P.M. Then, hearing that they might be prosecuted, they went to the executive committee of the Greensboro N.A.A.C.P. to ask advice.

"This was our first knowledge of this demonstration," said Dr. George C. Simkins, who is president of the organization. He said that he had then written to the New York headquarters of the Congress of Racial Equality, which is known as CORE. He requested assistance for the demonstrators, who numbered in the hundreds during the following days.

Dr. Simkins, a dentist, explained that he had heard of a successful attempt, led by CORE, to desegregate a Baltimore restaurant and had read one of the organization's pamphlets.

CORE'S field secretary, Gordon R. Carey, arrived from New York on Feb. 7. He said that he had assisted Negro students in some North Carolina cities after they had initiated the protests.

The Greensboro demonstrations and the others that it triggered were spontaneous, according to Mr. Carey. All of the Negroes questioned agreed on this.

The movement's chief targets were two national variety chains, S. H. Kress & Co. and the F. W. Woolworth Company. Other chains were affected. In some cities the students demonstrated at local stores.

The protests generally followed similar patterns. Young men and women and, in one case, high school boys and girls, walked into the stores and requested food service. Met with refusals in all cases, they remained at the lunch counters in silent protest.

The reaction of store managers in those instances was to close down the lunch counters and, when trouble developed or bomb threats were received, the entire store.

Hastily painted signs, posted on the counters, read: "Temporarily Closed," "Closed for Repairs," "Closed in the Interest of Public Safety," "No Trespassing," and "We Reserve The Right to Service the Public as We See Fit."

After a number of establishments had shut down in High Point, N. C., the S. H. Kress & Co. store remained open, its lunch counter desegregated. The secret? No stools.

Asked how long the store had been serving all comers on a stand-up basis, the manager replied, "I don't know. I just got transferred from Mississippi."

The demonstrations attracted crowds of whites. At first the hecklers were youths with duck-tailed haircuts. Some carried small Confederate battle flags. Later they were joined by older men in faded khakis and overalls.

The Negro youths were challenged to step outside and fight. Some of the remarks to the girls were jesting in nature, such as, "How about a date when we integrate?" Other remarks were not.

NEGRO KNOCKED DOWN

In a few cases the Negroes were elbowed, jostled and shoved. Itching powder was sprinkled on them and they were spattered with eggs.

At Rock Hill, S. C., a Negro youth was knocked from a stool by a white beside whom he sat. A bottle of ammonia was hurled through the door of a drug store there. The fumes brought tears to the eyes of the demonstrators.

The only arrests reported involved forty-three of the demonstrators. They were seized on a sidewalk outside a Woolworth store at a Raleigh shopping center. Charged with trespassing, they posted $50 bonds and were released.

The management of the shopping center contended that the sidewalk was private property.

In most cases, the demonstrators sat or stood at store counters talking in low voices, studying or staring impassively at their tormenters. There was little joking or smiling. Now and then a girl giggled nervously. Some carried bibles.

Those at Rock Hill were described by the local newspaper, The Evening Herald, as "orderly, polite, well-dressed and quiet."

'COMPLICATED HOSPITALITY'

Questions to their leaders about the reasons for the demonstrations drew such replies as: "We feel if we can spend our money on other goods we should be able to eat in the same establishments," "All I want is to come in and place my order and be served and leave a tip if I feel like it," and "This is definitely our purpose: integrated seating facilities with no isolated spots, no certain seats, but to sit wherever there is a vacancy."

Some newspapers noted the embarrassing position in which the variety chains found themselves. The News and Observer of Raleigh remarked editorially that in these stores the Negro was a guest who was cordially invited to the house but definitely not to the table. "And to say the least, this was complicated hospitality."

The newspaper said that to serve the Negroes might offend Southern whites while to do otherwise might result in the loss of the Negro trade.

"This business," it went on, "is causing headaches in New York and irritations in North Carolina. And somehow it revolves around the old saying that you can't have your chocolate cake and eat it too."

The Greensboro Daily News advocated that the lunch counters be closed or else opened on a desegregated basis.

North Carolina's Attorney General, Malcolm B. Seawell, asserted that the students were causing "irreparable harm" to relations between whites and Negroes.

Mayor William G. Enloe of Raleigh termed it "regrettable that some of our young Negro students would risk endangering these relations by seeking to change a long-standing custom in a manner that is all but destined to fail."

Some North Carolinians found it incomprehensible that the demonstrations were taking place in their state. They pointed to the progress made here toward desegregation of public facilities. A number of the larger cities in the Piedmont region, among them Greensboro, voluntarily accepted token desegregation of their schools after the Supreme Court's 1954 decisions.

But across the state there were indications that the Negro had weighed token desegregation and found it wanting.

When commenting on the subject, the Rev. F. L. Shuttlesworth of Birmingham, Ala., drew a chorus of "amens" from a packed N.A.A.C.P. meeting in a Greensboro church. "We don't want token freedom," he declared. "We want full freedom. What would a token dollar be worth?"

Warming to the subject, he shouted, "You educated us. You taught us to look up, white man. And we're looking up!"

Praising the demonstrators, he urged his listeners to be ready "to go to jail with Jesus" if necessary to "remove the dead albatross of segregation that makes America stink in the eyes of the world."

John H. Wheeler, a Negro lawyer who heads a Durham bank, said that the only difference among Negroes concerned the "when" and "how" of the attack on segregation. He contended that the question was whether the South would grant the minority race full citizenship status or commit economic suicide by refusing to do so.

The Durham Committee on Negro Affairs, which includes persons from many economic levels, pointed out in a statement that white officials had asked Negro leaders to stop the student demonstrations.

"It is our opinion," the statement said, "that instead of expressing disapproval, we have an obligation to support any peaceful movement which seeks to remove from the customs of our beloved Southland those unfair practices based upon race and color which have for so long a time been recognized as a stigma on our way of life and stumbling block to social and economic progress of the region."

It then asserted: "It is reasonable to expect that our state officials will recognize their responsibility for helping North Carolina live up to its reputation of being the enlightened, liberal and progressive state, which our industry hunters have been representing it to be."

The outlook for not only this state but also for the entire region is for increasing Negro resistance to segregation, according to Harold C. Fleming, executive director of the Southern Regional Council. The council is an interracial group of Southern leaders with headquarters in Atlanta. Its stated aim is the improvement of race relations.

"The lunch-counter 'sit-in,' " Mr. Fleming commented, "demonstrates something that the white community has been reluctant to face: the mounting determination of Negroes to be rid of all segregated barriers.

"Those who hoped that token legal adjustments to school desegregation would dispose of the racial issue are on notice to the contrary. We may expect more, not less, protests of this kind against enforced segregation in public facilities and services of all types."

Dr. King Favors Buyers' Boycott

BY CLAUDE SITTON | APRIL 16, 1960

RALEIGH, N. C., APRIL 15 — The Rev. Dr. Martin Luther King Jr. called today for a national "selective-buying" campaign against businesses that practice segregation.

He also urged the training of an elite group of volunteers for demonstrations against racial barriers. They would go to jail rather than pay fines levied because of their activities.

Dr. King made his recommendations in a statement at the opening of the first South-wide conference of Negro student leaders of the sit-in movement.

More than 100 students from forty Southern communities and ten states are attending the three-day session here on the campus of Shaw University. About ten white students, some of whom are from the North, also are taking part.

One of the white youths was attacked by an unidentified man earlier today while picketing downtown variety stores with a group of Negroes. He is John J. Northrup, a student at Colgate-Rochester Divinity School in Rochester, N. Y.

No policemen were present at the time of the assaults and no arrest had been made tonight on Mr. Northrup's complaint.

5 GROUPS TAKE PART

The conference is under the auspices of the Southern Christian Leadership Conference, which Dr. King heads. Cooperating organizations include the Congress of Racial Equality, the American Friends Service Committee, the National Student Association and the Fellowship of Reconciliation.

It was apparent that the students would lean heavily on Dr. King for advice in charting the strategy of the anti-segregation protests. The Atlanta minister headed the Montgomery, Ala., bus boycott.

In his statement Dr. King said that since the sit-in demonstrations began Feb. 1 in Greensboro, N. C., "more Negro freedom fighters have revealed to the nation and the world their determination and courage than has occurred in many years.

"They have embraced a philosophy of mass, direct, non-violent action. They are moving away from tactics which are suitable merely for gradual and long-term change."

Consideration of a nationwide campaign of selective buying was termed a "must" by him. Such a program "is a moral act," he said, continuing:

"It is a moral necessity to select, to buy from these agencies these stores and businesses where one can buy with dignity and self-respect. It is immoral to spend one's money where one cannot be treated with respect."

The training of volunteers who would go to jail, he contended, should be seriously considered.

14 Negroes Jailed in Atlanta Sit-Ins

BY THE NEW YORK TIMES | OCT. 20, 1960

ATLANTA, OCT. 19 — Fifty-one demonstrators, including the Rev. Dr. Martin Luther King Jr., were arrested here today during sit-in protests at downtown stores. Fourteen Negroes, including Dr. King, refused to post bond and went to jail.

The demonstrators, mostly college students, sought service at lunch counters in two department stores and eight variety stores. They also picketed four stores.

All the arrests took place at eating places in Rich's department store. Other stores closed their lunch counters.

City Court judges were holding the demonstrators for County Court under bond. The defendants, arraigned in groups, were refusing to post bond, saying they would stay in jail until tried.

The defendants pleaded not guilty to a charge of refusing to leave private property when requested, based on a statute passed this year.

Dr. King, offered bond, said he would refuse it and stay in jail a year or ten years if necessary. In court, he declared:

"We did nothing wrong in going to Rich's today." He said the, object of the demonstrations was to bring the whole issue of desegregation into the "conscience of Atlanta."

Dr. King's appearance as a demonstrator among college students was new. The pastor, who previously led the successful bus boycott in Montgomery, Ala., came to Atlanta early this year.

Demonstrators, he said, went "peacefully, nonviolently, in a deep spirit of love."

The stores at which no arrests occurred were the Davison-Paxon department store, an affiliate of Macy's, Inc., New York, and branches of the Newberry, H. L. Green, F. W. Woolworth, W. T. Grant, Kress and McCrory chains.

DONALD UHRBROCK/THE LIFE IMAGES COLLECTION/GETTY IMAGES

The Rev. Dr. Martin Luther King Jr. strategizing with a group of college-student sit-in organizers in his office.

None of these had experienced demonstrations before. Rich's has been the target of a concentrated campaign of sit-ins most of the year at its four all-white eating places.

The Woolworth, Grant, Kress and McCrory-McLellan chains announced yesterday that they had integrated lunch counters in 112 cities in the South, none in Georgia.

The arrests at Rich's occurred sporadically, mostly in the store's largest dining room. They came after Frank Nealy, chairman of the store's board, and other officials replied affirmatively when asked by city detectives if they desired that demonstrators leave and the demonstrators then refused.

The demonstration followed a week-end meeting here of the Students Nonviolent Coordinating Committee.

Normally it takes several weeks for cases bound over from City Court to reach trial in County Court.

Dr. King Is Jailed in Traffic Case

BY THE NEW YORK TIMES | OCT. 26, 1960

DECATUR, GA., OCT. 25 — The Rev. Martin Luther King Jr. was ordered today to serve four months in prison. A judge here ruled that his participation in an Atlanta sit-in demonstration had violated the terms of a suspended sentence in a traffic case. The probation was based on non-violation of a state or Federal law for a year. Dr. King and a number of students were arrested last week after a sit-in demonstration at Rich's Department Store. Store officials have said they will not press the charges. Court and prison officials indicated that Dr. King would be transferred to a state prison immediately to begin serving today's sentence.

Judge Oscar Mitchell of DeKalb Civil and Criminal Court ordered the suspended sentence revoked after a hearing that was attended by about 200 persons, including Roy Wilkins, executive secretary of the National Association for the Advancement of Colored People. Judge Mitchell had ordered Dr. King into court to show cause why his arrest in the sit-in demonstration was not a reason for putting the suspended sentence into effect. The sentence was for twelve months. It was suspended when Dr. King paid a $25 fine last month on a charge of driving without a Georgia driver's license.

The judge said after today's hearing that an appeal bond could not be obtained in a revocation-of-probation case such as Dr. King's. D. L. Hollowell, who represented Dr. King in the hearing, said such bond was discretionary with the judge.

He said that, if appeal and bond on the revocation were denied at a hearing set for tomorrow morning before Judge Mitchell, he would ask for the release of Dr. King on bond pending an appeal of the original traffic case.

He said an appeal in that case was filed on Monday.

A spokesman for the Georgia Corrections Department said tonight that he had assigned Dr. King to the Georgia State Prison at Reidsville, the state's largest prison. The prison sentence ended a dramatic day in Georgia's integration struggle. It began with Dr. King's being taken from one jail to another to await the hearing. Handcuffed, he passed before a praying group of white Southern theologians, here from Northern schools on a mission of encouragement for sit-ins.

Dr. King's main defense at the hearing was that a Georgia law under which he was arrested during the sit-ins is unconstitutional. He also argued that the original twelve-month traffic sentence was twice as long as the law allowed.

The status of Dr. King's sit-in arrest was brought into the hearing. The store's decision not to press the charges is in line with an agreement for a thirty-day truce in the sit-in campaign in Atlanta.

Mayor William B. Hartsfield had this comment on today's developments:

"I have no desire to criticize the courts. But I have made requests of all the news agencies that in their stories they make it clear that this hearing did not take place in Atlanta, Ga."

Gov. Ernest Vandiver was not available for comment. His executive secretary, Peter Zack Geer, said:

"I think the maximum sentence for Martin Luther King might do him good, might make a law-abiding citizen out of him and teach him to respect the law of Georgia."

The Congress of Racial Equality called the sentencing of Dr. King yesterday a "gross miscarriage of justice."

The organization protested the sentence in a telegram to President Eisenhower and Attorney General William P. Rogers.

CHAPTER 2

From Protest to Jail and Back

Dr. King's inspirational rhetoric, oratorical style and insistence on nonviolent protest moved thousands of people to participate in marches, rallies, sit-ins and boycotts. Many, including Dr. King, were arrested. Far from suppressing the protests, however, the arrests helped them grow stronger.

Dr. King, Symbol Of the Segregation Struggle

BY CLAUDE SITTON | JAN. 22, 1961

ATLANTA — In a brief five years, a young Baptist minister has emerged from relative obscurity to a position of power and prominence in the struggle against racial codes and customs.

Not since the days of Booker T. Washington, has a Southern Negro so attracted public attention. Chiefs of state have sought his counsel and would-be chiefs of state his favor. Hundreds of thousands of persons have flocked to hear him blend emotion and logic in a skillful appeal for interracial justice. Although he has only just turned 32, he has been showered with praise and honor far beyond the expectations of most men twice his age.

Yet, he is also the object of bitter hatred, particularly among the whites of his region. The Governor of Georgia, his native state, has declared him unwanted, unwelcome, a man to be watched. Many who sympathize with his goals consider his methods dangerously provocative. Even some Negroes regard him as a pious interloper, bent on personal aggrandizement.

But on one point his friends and enemies generally agree: the Rev. Dr. Martin Luther King is the symbol today of the fight to end segregation.

Neither fame nor controversy is evident in King's appearance. He is a small man. A broad, sloping face and heavily muscled neck and shoulders lend his 5-foot-8 frame an aspect of physical power. But this impression is largely destroyed by his expressive, almost delicate hands, his almond-shaped eyes and his air of pensive detachment.

Only when he stands in the pulpit or at the speaker's lectern does the full force of his personality become apparent. His delivery, while restrained, is nonetheless moving. His thoughts flow as smoothly as his rich baritone voice. In the fabric of his message, the warp is reason, the woof persuasion, colored by an admixture of irony and pathos, interspersed with quotes from the great philosophers and bound by the strong thread of conviction.

At ease in his shirtsleeves in the modest, rented frame house where he lives with his attractive wife, Coretta, and their 5-year-old daughter and 3-year-old son, Martin King seems calm and self-assured. There is no arrogance about him, no intellectual posturing. He voices no bitterness against the whites who have handled him roughly.

BUT THIS gentle manner cloaks a core of steel, for King is a social actionist who believes that "creative, instructive tension is necessary for the birth of a new society." He is a zealot whose goal is the destruction of the system that "gives the segregator a false sense of superiority and the segregated a false sense of inferiority."

King comes by the role naturally. His mother's father, the Rev. A. D. Williams, turned Ebenezer Baptist Church into one of the leading houses of worship for Atlanta Negroes. He also led a boycott against an inflammatory newspaper owned by a white, Northern chain. It soon disappeared from the scene. Today, King and his father serve as co-pastors of the church.

King has been an active servant in the cause of integration almost since he left Boston University in 1954 with a doctorate in systematic theology. He had little more than arrived in Montgomery, Ala., to fill his first pastorate when the bus boycott there began in December 1955.

A Federal court desegregation order, rather than the boycott, ended the dispute in December 1956. Nevertheless, the participation of most of the city's 50,000 Negroes in the movement, and, perhaps, the climate of the times, made it a benchmark in the segregation controversy.

King had taken no part in the decision to organize the boycott, but for several reasons he was tapped to be head of the Montgomery Improvement Association, which was set up to guide the movement. For one thing, as a minister, he was less subject to economic pressures than, say, a Negro business man would have been. For another, as a newcomer to Montgomery, he had not become identified with any faction — or dispute — within the Negro community.

King accepted rather reluctantly. Much of the planning and administration of the boycott was conducted by the association's board of directors, but it was the young pastor's oratory that inspired the rank-and-file to stay on the sidewalks and off the buses. And it was his influence that prevented Negroes from exacting retribution from the whites after his home had been bombed.

Throughout the boycott, King displayed an uncommon talent for articulating the aspirations of his people. When it had ended, it was clear that the struggle had provided the Southern Negro with one of his most eloquent and effective spokesmen. But it had done more than that.

WHILE STUDYING at Crozer Theological Seminary in Chester, Pa., and at Boston University, King had become interested in the principle of civil disobedience expounded by Thoreau and Gandhi. The boycott gave him an opportunity to field-test his modified version of passive resistance and nonviolence as a weapon against segregation. He set down his findings in a personalized account of the Montgomery struggle, the book "Stride Toward Freedom."

Stated simply by King, passive resistance means a willingness to suffer and sacrifice. "It may mean going to jail. If such is the case, the resister must be willing to fill the jail houses of the South. It may even mean physical death. But if physical death is the price that a man must pay to free his children and his white brethren from a permanent death of the spirit, then nothing could be more redemptive."

THERE IS A corollary message for whites, which the minister repeats frequently in his speeches.

"We will match your capacity to inflict suffering with our capacity to endure suffering. We will meet your physical force with soul force. We will not hate you, but we cannot in all good conscience obey your unjust laws .... But we will soon wear you down by our capacity to suffer. And in winning our freedom we will so appeal to your heart and conscience that we will win you in the process."

It might be said that this philosophy meets the test of the pragmatist in one important respect. Any attempt by the Southern Negro to mount a violent attack against segregation would bring down upon him the full weight of white-controlled law enforcement with disastrous consequences. "Our oppressors would be happy if we resorted to violence," King says.

As a result of his role in the boycott, King found himself deluged with requests for public appearances. He has seized that opportunity to press the cause of integration, traveling thousands of miles by air each year and journeying to Europe, India and Africa. Citizens of newly emerging African nations have welcomed him as a fellow soldier in the fight for freedom. And so he considers himself.

"A great revolution is taking place in our world, a social revolution in the minds and souls of men. And it has been transformed into a unified voice, crying out, 'We want to be free.' "

NOT LONG AFTER the end of the boycott, King and his followers organized the Southern Christian Leadership Conference. This federation of anti-segregation groups serves as a clearing house for information and strategy and as a collector of funds.

"The conference," King says, "has as its foremost emphasis the philosophy of nonviolence — to spread the philosophy of nonviolence and to demonstrate through action its operational techniques."

For a time, it seemed doubtful that the conference would amount to much. The Negro effort had been largely concentrated in the courts and, to a much lesser extent, in the fields of information, education and voter registration. Here, the long-established professionals of the National Association for the Advancement of Colored People were preeminent.

Liberals had hoped the conference would become a training ground for new leadership, sorely needed in smaller cities and rural areas to help Negroes take advantage of rights already secured through litigation. But like so many other groups of its kind, the S.C.L.C. showed a weakness for issuing statements, conducting conferences and scheduling dramatic but ineffective demonstrations.

The shortcomings of the conference may be caused in part by its small staff and the heavy demands made upon King's time by his other duties. But his lack of enthusiasm for administration would seem to be a factor. In a biography entitled "Crusader Without Violence," L. D. Reddick notes that "King is more at home with a conception than he is with the details of its application."

The opportunity for the S.C.L.C. to translate thought into action came with the outbreak of the sit-in demonstrations. King and his colleagues saw the movement as a refutation of the old contention that the Negro was satisfied with segregation — or with token desegregation. He said at the outset that the students, "through their suffering and sacrifice, may be able to arouse the dozing conscience of the South and America."

THE FOUR STUDENTS who participated in the first protest on Feb. 2, 1960, in a Greensboro, N. C., variety store were unsure of their tactics and their legal position. Seeking aid and advice, they turned to the N.A.A.C.P. and then to the Congress of Racial Equality (CORE).

CORE, an interracial group formed in 1943, had pioneered the sit-in technique in the United States. The N.A.A.C.P. had employed it on a limited basis. It is often over-looked that both continued to advise sit-in demonstrators in a number of Southern cities, some of which led the way in desegregating their lunch counters.

The students, however, needed a spokesman and a regional organization that could coordinate their activities and pass information from one city to another. Because of his youth, his intellectual appeal and his status as leader of the Montgomery boycott, King appeared an ideal candidate.

Furthermore, the S.C.L.C. moved swiftly to stake out a claim in the new field. It brought the student leaders together at Raleigh, N. C., to establish the Student Nonviolent Coordinating Committee. Although the students have continued to exercise considerable independence, their committee now operates in Atlanta as a virtual adjunct of the S.C.L.C.

As a result of these developments, there has been some conflict between the N.A.A.C.P. and the S.C.L.C. Roy Wilkins, executive secretary of the older organization, and King have sought to hold it to a minimum. But some of the more ambitious men in the S.C.L.C. have made no secret of their scorn for the association, calling it the "black bourgeois club" — and worse.

In many respects, the sit-ins have provided the sternest test yet for King. His own participation in an Atlanta demonstration landed him in jail after he refused to post bond on charges of breaking a new anti-trespass law. The charges were dropped as a result of Mayor William B. Hartsfield's efforts. But a judge in suburban DeKalb County revoked King's probation, previously imposed for driving without a Georgia license, and the pastor was hauled off to the state prison for a day before being freed pending an appeal.

THE INCIDENT took place at the height of the Presidential campaign. It brought a sympathy call to Mrs. King from John F. Kennedy and another to the DeKalb County judge from Robert Kennedy, his brother. There is considerable evidence that the calls enhanced the Democratic nominee's standing with Negro voters, while the stint behind bars increased King's stature as a Negro leader.

King still faces the very real possibility that he will have to spend four months at hard labor. While he would welcome a jail term for breaking the anti-trespass law, time served for a traffic violation would be another matter indeed.

The minister did not become an advocate of law violation without considerable thought. His position today is this: "I say obey the law when the law is right, when the law is just and when the law is in line with the moral law of the universe. When conscience tells someone that a law is unjust, then I think a righteous man has no alternative but to conscientiously disobey that law."

It is his view that the law-breaker does not seek to defy or to evade the law, but willingly accepts the penalty in order to convince its makers that the law is wrong. "The individual who disobeys the law in a loving spirit and accepts the consequences is dignifying the law."

He contends that Socrates, the early Christians, the members of the Boston Tea Party, the abolitionists and those who opposed Hitler's rise to power all practiced civil disobedience. By the same token, he concedes the right of sincere whites to oppose desegregation as long as that opposition takes a nonviolent form.

This doctrine has its dangers, as King is aware. Probably the strongest influence for compliance with the 1954 school desegregation ruling of the Supreme Court has been the oft-repeated statement that it is the law of the land and therefore must be obeyed. This argument would get short shrift by King's standards.

Few would deny the right of Negroes to boycott establishments that practice segregation. But some whites argue that King is on shaky ground when he in turn criticizes the Citizens Councils for using this weapon to maintain segregation.

THE PASTOR also has noted that the councils, while piously abhorring violence, actually create an atmosphere in which violence thrives. King's critics contend that the sit-in demonstrations have the same effect. His answer is that trouble, almost without fail, has been started by whites opposing the protests.

There are serious doubts as to the depth of understanding that King's followers have of civil disobedience, particularly the willingness to submit to the penalties of the law. Undeniably, some of the students show a sketchy knowledge at best of the process.

The demonstrations have damaged the moral cause of the Negro in some circles heretofore sympathetic. "King has made the Negro liable to being called the offender rather than the offended," contends a moderate newspaper editor. "I am disturbed that the emotionalism over the issue could so carry Americans away that they could be uncritical of the law-breaking aspect. I think this is unhealthy."

Liberals who agree with King have been distressed by his inadequate defense in public debate of the nonviolent technique. "He has both the strengths and weaknesses of a great preacher," says one man. "One of the weaknesses is that when you are thrown on the bare rocks of intellectual argument you fail."

Nevertheless, King and passive resistance have become inextricably interwoven with the present and the future of Southern race relations, although the pastor concedes that many Negroes are not prepared for the ordeals and sacrifices that it requires.

LOOKING TO the future, King sees white massive resistance to desegregation — exemplified recently in Louisiana — ending within five years. With the exception of a few rural areas, he predicts, legal segregation will be wiped out within fifteen years. And substantial progress will have been made toward true integration by the turn of the century. But the chief burden of fulfilling this timetable falls on the Negro.

"Even a superficial look at history," Martin Luther King has written, "reveals that no social advance rolls in on the wheels of inevitability. Every step toward the goal of justice requires sacrifice, suffering, and struggle; the tireless exertions and passionate concern of dedicated individuals."

Dr. King's 3 Children Visit Him; He Is Allowed Out of Jail Cell

BY HEDRICK SMITH | AUG. 6, 1962

ALBANY, GA., AUG. 5 — The Rev. Dr. Martin Luther King Jr. received a visit in jail today from his three small children.

They had not seen their father for almost a month because he has been busy with the desegregation campaign here. But their parting was cheerful.

It was the first time they had called on their father during one of his frequent periods in jail in recent years.

"The children have known all along that he was in jail," said their mother, Mrs. Coretta King.

"They knew he was not going to be able to come back with them. They didn't cry when they left him. They accepted it," she said.

PREPARED FOR VISIT

Their acceptance reflected patient and careful preparation by Mrs. King, who is a soft-spoken woman.

Before the visit, Mrs. King seemed concerned about the children's reaction. She said her husband "didn't want them to see him in the cell."

"So the police let him come out to a shoe-shine stand near the front of the jail."

Mrs. King wore a white, pleated dress and a pearl necklace and earrings for the fifteen-minute visit. Her daughter, Yolanda, almost 7 years old, was dressed in a sun suit, and the two boys, Martin Luther 3d, 4, and Dexter, 18 months old, wore plaid shorts and white shirts.

They entered the jail about 1 P.M., accompanied by Mrs. Rachel Ward, a parishioner at Dr. King's church in Atlanta, and the Rev. Wyatt Tee Walker, an aide to Dr. King from the Southern Christian Leadership Conference.

After the visit, the children frolicked in the foyer of City Hall while Mrs. King talked with newsmen. She said her husband was in good spirits.

"He looks well. I think he feels much better after seeing the children. It gave him a lift," she said.

Mrs. King said that for the past two years she had explained to her children why their father went to jail.

"I said, 'Daddy's gone to jail to help people. They don't have good homes to live in. They don't have enough food. Daddy would like all the people to have these things."

"I said, 'He's gone to jail to help the people get these things.' This is all I told them because I didn't think they'd understand things like freedom."

The children grew slowly to accept the explanation, she said.

Dr. King is awaiting trial next week for his part in a demonstration July 27. With other members of the Albany movement, he was seeking a meeting with the City Commissioner to discuss racial problems here.

Mrs. King said her daughter had cried: "I want to see Daddy, I want him to come home."

When Mrs. King explained that Dr. King was helping other Negro people, Yolanda replied, "Oh, yeah, tell him to stay there until he fixes it so I can go to Funtown."

Funtown is a segregated amusement park in Atlanta.

Birmingham Jails 1,000 More Negroes

BY CLAUDE SITTON | MAY 7, 1963

BIRMINGHAM, ALA., MAY 6 — About 1,000 Negroes were arrested today as wave after wave of marchers chanted challenges to segregation.

The arrest total, an estimate from the police, was the highest for a single day in the five-week racial crisis in this Southern steel center. The authorities said about 40 per cent of those arrested were juveniles.

Approximately 100 policemen and firemen held a sullen crowd of more than 2,000 Negroes in check at the 16th Street Baptist Church, departure point for the marchers. They were assisted by ministers who emerged from the church to plead against violence.

5 SUBDUE NEGRO WOMAN

A Negro woman who resisted a policeman's attempt to force her off a sidewalk was wrestled to the pavement by five patrolmen, one of whom pinned her down with a knee in her neck. A Negro man ripped a policeman's shirt and sought to wrest his revolver from him. Both Negroes were subdued and carried to jail in patrol wagons.

Policemen drove motorcycles down sidewalks in the vicinity of the church and the Kelly Ingram Park to clear away bystanders. Although firemen stood by at pumper trucks with high-pressure nozzles and hoses at the ready, the order to use them never came.

Dick Gregory, 35-year-old Chicago comedian, led the first group of 19 marchers from the church. They were quickly arrested. The last wave followed Barbara Deming, a white woman, out of the church an hour and ten minutes later. Miss Deming, who identified herself as a writer for The Nation magazine, also was arrested.

Estimates from the police and Negro leaders indicated that 200 to 225 of the prisoners had been arrested in the downtown area while picketing outside department, drug and variety stores.

Many of both groups carried toothbrushes in their pockets in anticipation of their arrest.

The Negroes plan further mass demonstrations tomorrow, according to one of their leaders.

Meanwhile, negotiations to resolve the controversy reached a stalemate. "In fact, they never really got started," a Negro leader asserted.

Burke Marshall, chief of the Justice Department's civil rights division, continued his efforts, under orders from Attorney General Robert F. Kennedy, to persuade white and Negro leaders to reach agreement.

Mr. Marshall conferred for two and a half hours this morning at a private home with the Rev. Dr. Martin Luther King Jr., of Atlanta, president of the Southern Christian Leadership Conference. Their talk was largely fruitless, according to a source close to the integration leader.

This source said the city's official, business, and civic leadership had refused to meet any of the Negroes' desegregation demands at the present time. This view was confirmed by whites in high positions.

There were at least two meetings yesterday between Negro leaders and an unofficial committee of the Chamber of Commerce headed by Sidney Smyer, a leading Birmingham real estate dealer, and others.

There were further meetings tonight among leaders of the Negro and white communities. Reports were that additional concessions had been offered if Dr. King and the local leaders would call a halt to the present demonstrations until after the new city administration was confirmed in office.

'TOO LITTLE, TOO LATE'

Negro sources indicated that the compromise on desegregation that had been offered was "too little and too late."

In Atlanta yesterday Dr. King expressed hope that there would be some action on the part of the Birmingham "white power structure." He made the statement before he received a report on negotiations here. Dr. King returned to Birmingham on an early plane this morning.

It was not known whether Mr. Marshall was sitting in on the meetings of the two sides. He has been in touch with several leaders of both the Negro and the white community and he met for two hours last night with the Rev. A. D. King, a younger brother of Dr. King. A. D. King is minister of a church in suburban Ensley and one of the local leaders of the desegregation campaign.

Minimum demands of the desegregation leaders have been removal of racial restriction in downtown snack bars, public facilities and stores, adoption of nonracial hiring practices for such posts as sales girls and secretaries and formation of a bi-racial committee to carry on continuing negotiations for further desegregation.

All this could be done, Negro leaders say, without official city government action. Promises on all these things were made last fall and then not fulfilled, they charged.

Dr. King, his lieutenants and officials of the Alabama Christian Movement for Human Rights, a conference affiliate, apparently drew heavily today on Negro schools for demonstrators.

FLYERS URGE ACTION

A flyer distributed by their supporters urged:

"Fight for freedom first then go to school."

It continued:

"Join the thousands in jail who are making their witness for freedom. Come to the 16th Street Baptist Church now … and we'll soon be free. It's up to you to free our teachers, our parents, yourself and our country."

At least one Negro woman disagreed with this philosophy. She raced after one group of marchers, seized a teen-age girl by the arm and dragged her out of the line.

This action brought a chorus of boos from the crowd of negro spectators. The police finally took the two and the man who was with them out of the crowd and into the safety of a nearby park.

As groups of Negroes streamed out of the church before noon, one official in the movement said they were going to schools to ask students to join the marches.

The Birmingham News reported that one Negro educator said his school had 1,339 students absent and only 87 present.

The juveniles are being held either at the Boys Home or in the 4-H Club building at the fair grounds. With those arrested today, the total number of both adults and juveniles in custody is estimated at 2,425. Authorities say they are unable to provide an accurate count.

There is no lack of space for more, according to Eugene Connor, Commissioner of Fire, Police and Education in one of Birmingham's two city governments. The dispute over which government is legal is in the courts.

"All right," Mr. Connor said as the police loaded demonstrators into patrol wagons and school buses, "you-all send them on over there. I got plenty of room in the jail."

Mr. Connor, in shirtsleeves with a straw hat cocked over one eye, watched the eager young marchers, some of whom ran to the waiting patrol wagons.

"Boy, if that's religion, I don't want any," he said.

"Freedom! Freedom! Freedom!" chanted the Negro girls and boys as the school buses swept by the commissioner on the way to jail.

"If you'd ask half of them what freedom means, they couldn't tell you," asserted Mr. Connor.

The day was hot and muggy as Negroes began to gather on the sidewalks along 16th Street and Sixth Avenue across from Kelly Ingram Park. Some spectators took up positions in the windows of the Jockey Boy restaurant or the steps of the church.

The mass rally already had begun in the yellow brick church.

The police made their first attempt to clear the streets and sidewalks in the area of the church shortly after 12:30 P.M., and then brought up three red pumpers whose crews hooked up hoses and stood waiting for orders.

Some 15 minutes later, Dr. King and his aides arrived. Mr. Gregory, who had made several brief visits to the church, returned after talking to Negroes along the street in an attempt to discourage them from breaching the nonviolent pattern that Dr. King has sought to enforce.

SEEKS ASSURANCES

The Rev. James Bevel of Cleveland, Miss., a Leadership Conference field representative, then left the church and sought assurance from a police captain that the fire hoses would not be used on the marchers when they emerged. He offered his hand to the officer, who declined with a smile to shake it.

"I think you've had enough experience with us to know that we are not going to use any more force than necessary," the captain told Mr. Bevel.

The minister returned to the church and a few minutes later Mr. Gregory, dressed in a gray suit of Italian cut, walked out at the head of 19 boys and girls.

"Everybody wants freedom," asserted the placard he held.

"Don't mind walking, 'cause I want my freedom now," chanted the marchers.

Police Capt. George Wall, wearing a white World War I-type helmet, stood waiting for the marchers in front of the office of Painters Union Local 57, holding an electric bull horn.

"You're leading this parade?" he asked Mr. Gregory, who said that he was. The official then advised the marchers that they were violating a city parade ordinance and a state court injunction against such demonstrations.

"Do you understand?" asked Captain Wall.

"No I don't," replied the comedian in a somewhat more subdued manner than that which he had used in his confrontations with Greenwood, Miss., police during voter registration demonstrations there.

The captain ran through the formalities again and asked the marchers if they wished to disperse, Mr. Gregory said they did not.

"Dick Gregory says they will not disperse," announced the captain over the bull horn. "Call the wagon." This was the first group arrested.

MORE MARCHERS

Even before this exchange had been completed, two other groups of marchers already were waiting at the end of the line and for the next hour they kept coming in groups of 20, 30, 40 and 50.

Two or three groups switched the procedure by walking away from the waiting patrol wagons and school buses, circling the block in front of the church and submitting to arrest on the opposite side of the park. Another group was picked up by the police while kneeling on the sidewalk a block away.

Meanwhile, ministers were standing on the church steps waving other prospective demonstrators into the church. There, Dr. King stressed and restressed the need for a nonviolent approach with the admonition, "The world is watching you."

As one group stepped off the curb and started across Sixth Avenue, two patrolmen stepped out with their nightsticks and gently cut off a little boy bringing up the rear who appeared to be less than 5 years old.

Chanting their freedom songs, the Negroes marched gaily toward the waiting police as older Negroes watching from the porches along the line of march applauded or sang softly a verse from "We Shall Overcome":

"Black and white together.

"We shall overcome some day."

Shortly after two o'clock, a bottle came sailing from among the Negro bystanders and smashed on the pavement near the police.

Minutes later a minister emerged from the church and began urging those outside, "We want everybody in the church."

Heavy police reinforcements had been brought up and patrolmen and auxiliary policemen began clearing sidewalks and streets in the vicinity.

At about 2:40 P. M. a man rushed out of the church shouting "It's all over, it's all over for today." The remaining stragglers were joined by the hundreds within the church and walked slowly away, breaking up into small groups as they reached the business district four blocks away.

"I Have a Dream . . ."

BY JAMES RESTON | AUG. 29, 1963

WASHINGTON, AUG. 28 — Abraham Lincoln, who presided in his stone temple today above the children of the slaves he emancipated, may have used just the right words to sum up the general reaction to the Negro's massive march on Washington. "I think," he wrote to Gov. Andrew G. Curtin of Pennsylvania in 1861, "the necessity of being ready increases. Look to it." Washington may not have changed a vote today, but is a little more conscious tonight of the necessity of being ready for freedom. It may not "look to it" at once, since it is looking to so many things, but it will be a long time before it forgets the melodious and melancholy voice of the Rev. Dr. Martin Luther King Jr crying out his dreams to the multitude.

It was Dr. King who, near the end of the day, touched the vast audience. Until then the pilgrimage was merely a great spectacle. Only those marchers from the embattled towns in the Old Confederacy had anything like the old crusading zeal. For many the day seemed an adventure, a long outing in the late summer sun — part liberation from home, part Sunday School picnic, part political convention, and part fish-fry.

But Dr. King brought them alive in the late afternoon with a peroration that was an anguished echo from all the old American reformers. Roger Williams calling for religious liberty, Sam Adams calling for political liberty, old man Thoreau denouncing coercion, William Lloyd Garrison demanding emancipation, and Eugene V. Debs crying for economic equality — Dr. King echoed them all.

"I have a dream," he cried again and again. And each time the dream was a promise out of our ancient articles of faith: phrases from the Constitution, lines from the great anthem of the nation, guarantees from the Bill of Rights, all ending with a vision that they might one day all come true.

FIND JOURNEY WORTHWHILE

Dr. King touched all the themes of the day, only better than anybody else. He was full of the symbolism of Lincoln and Gandhi, and the cadences of the Bible. He was both militant and sad, and he sent the crowd away feeling that the long journey had been worthwhile.

This demonstration impressed political Washington because it combined a number of things no politician can ignore. It had the force of numbers. It had the melodies of both the church and the theater. And it was able to invoke the principles of the founding fathers to rebuke the inequalities and hypocrisies of modern American life.

There was a paradox in the day's performance. The Negro leaders demanded equality "now," while insisting that this was only the "beginning" of the struggle. Yet it was clear that the "now," which appeared on almost every placard on Constitution Avenue, was merely an opening demand, while the exhortation to increase the struggle was what was really on the leaders' minds.

The question of the day, of course, was raised by Dr. King's theme: Was this all a dream or will it help the dream come true?

No doubt this vast effort helped the Negro drive against discrimination. It was better covered by television and the press than any event here since President Kennedy's inauguration, and, since indifference is almost as great a problem to the Negro as hostility, this was a plus.

None of the dreadful things Washington feared came about. The racial hooligans were scarce. Even the local Nazi, George Lincoln Rockwell, minded his manners, which is an extraordinary innovation for him. And there were fewer arrests than any normal day for Washington, probably because all the saloons and hootch peddlers were closed.

POLITICIANS ARE IMPRESSED

The crowd obviously impressed the politicians. The presence of nearly a quarter of a million petitioners anywhere always makes a Senator think. He seldom ignores that many potential votes, and it did not escape the notice of Congressmen that these Negro organizations, some of which had almost as much trouble getting out a crowd as the Washington Senators several years ago, were now capable of organizing the largest demonstrating throng ever gathered at one spot in the District of Columbia.

It is a question whether this rally raised too many hopes among the Negroes or inspired the Negroes here to work harder for equality when they got back home. Most observers here think the latter is true, even though all the talk of "Freedom NOW" and instant integration is bound to lead to some disappointment.

The meetings between the Negro leaders on the one hand and President Kennedy and the Congressional leaders on the other also went well and probably helped the Negro cause. The Negro leaders were careful not to seem to be putting improper pressure on Congress. They made no specific requests or threats, but they argued their case in small groups and kept the crowd off Capitol Hill.

Whether this will win any new votes for the civil rights and economic legislation will probably depend on the over-all effect of the day's events on the television audience.

THE MAJOR IMPONDERABLE

This is the major imponderable of the day. The speeches were varied and spotty. Like their white political brethren, the Negroes cannot run a political meeting without letting everybody talk. Also, the platform was a bedlam of moving figures who seemed to be interested in everything except listening to the speaker. This distracted the audience.

Nevertheless, Dr. King and Roy Wilkins, head of the National Association for the Advancement of Colored People, and one or two others got the message across. James Baldwin, the author, summed up the day succinctly. The day was important in itself, he said, and "what we do with this day is even more important."

He was convinced that the country is finally grappling with the

Negro problem instead of evading it; that the Negro himself was "for the first time" aware of his value as a human being and was "no longer at the mercy of what the white people imagine the Negro to be."

MERELY THE BEGINNING

On the whole, the speeches were not calculated to make Republican politicians very happy with the Negro. This may hurt, for, without substantial Republican support, the Kennedy program on civil rights and jobs is not going through.

Apparently this point impressed President Kennedy, who listened to some of the speeches on television. When the Negro leaders came out of the White House, Dr. King emphasized that bipartisan support was essential for passage of the Kennedy civil rights program.

Aside from this, the advantages of the day for the Negro cause outran the disadvantages. Above all, they got over Lincoln's point that "the necessity of being ready increases." For they left no doubt that this was not the climax of their campaign for equality but merely the beginning, that they were going to stay in the streets until they could get equality in the schools, restaurants, houses and employment agencies of the nation, and that, as they demonstrated here today, they had found an effective way to demonstrate for changes in the laws without breaking the law themselves.

Dr. King Urges Nonviolence in Rights Protests

BY GENE CURRIVAN | MARCH 15, 1964

THE REV. DR. MARTIN LUTHER KING JR. predicted yesterday there would be enormous civil rights demonstrations throughout the country. He urged that they be nonviolent.

Violence, he said, would play into the hands of "many opponents in the South who would be happy if we turned to violence."

Dr. King's call for "disciplined" demonstrations was made in an interview before he spoke to more than 2,500 members of the United Federation of Teachers at their spring luncheon in the Americana Hotel.

In his speech, Dr. King, who is president of the Southern Christian Leadership Conference, said that race relations had reached a crisis but he was certain that "the white majority was willing to meet the Negro half-way."

His advocacy of nonviolence was a stand opposite that taken by Malcolm X, leader of the Black nationalists, who believes that violence is the only language the white man understands. He characterized Malcom X's "call to arms" as "ineffective and immoral."

Dr. King said that he would probably talk to Malcolm X and try to dissuade him.

"Actually," he said, "I dislike to discuss violence because sometimes discussion itself leads to it. I believe that the struggle ahead will be of massive proportions but it will be nonviolent and disciplined because the Negro, not necessarily all Negroes, have come to see that nonviolence is the best strategy."

He contended that the white people had misjudged the mood of the Negro.

DOORSTEP SIT-INS URGED

"It is one of frustration and determination but this determination does not have to express itself in violence," he said.

As to the Senate debate on the civil rights bill, Dr. King thought those favoring the bill should "wear down the filibusterers."

He suggested "dramatic community filibusters" to draw attention to the issues and, if necessary, sit-ins on the doorsteps of some Congressmen "to expose them to the nation." On the New York scene, Dr. King said he thought the school boycott was an effective weapon to call attention to "injustices and indignities" but he insisted that it should be well organized.

He told the teachers that "poor quality and segregated education will not be overcome without some cost to the white majority."

"It would be pleasant if it could be painless," he added, "but there are no miracles. Many people who object to necessary change are inherently against desegregation. However, many others who have opposed change are not for segregation. They are opposed to inconvenience for their children.

"It must be understood that Negro parents are fighting for the deepest needs of grossly deprived children. They are trying to loosen the manacles of the ghetto from the hands of their children."

Charles Cogen, president of the federation, presented Dr. King with the John Dewey Award, which is conferred annually to outstanding citizens who have aided education.

Martin Luther King Jr. Awarded Nobel Peace Prize

BY INTERNATIONAL HERALD TRIBUNE | OCT. 15, 1964

THE REV. DR. MARTIN LUTHER KING, the 35-year-old American Negro leader, today [Oct. 14] was awarded the 1964 Nobel Peace Prize for his "consistent support" of the principle of nonviolence in the Negro campaign for civil rights. He said he would use the 273,000 Swedish crowns prize (about $53,000) to strengthen the civil rights campaign in the United States. Dr. King is the 12th American to receive the prize. He is the second Negro leader to win in four years. The 1960 award was given to Albert Luthuli, of South Africa. A third Negro, Dr. Ralph J. Bunche, of the United States, was the 1950 winner. Dr. King, whose fight against racial discrimination has brought him many jail terms, will receive the prize at Oslo University on Dec. 10. "I do not consider this merely an honor to me personally, but a tribute to the discipline, wise restraint and majestic courage of the millions of gallant Negro and white persons of good will who have followed a nonviolent course in seeking to establish a reign of justice and a rule of love across this nation of ours," he said. Dr. King was selected from a list proposed by former Peace Prize winners, members of governments and parliaments around the world and other dignitaries.

67 Negroes Jailed in Alabama Drive

BY JOHN HERBERS | JAN. 20, 1965

SELMA, ALA., JAN. 19 — A group of Negroes who have been trying to register to vote refused today to return to a courthouse alley assigned to them and wound up in jail.

Sheriff James G. Clark arrested 62 on a charge of unlawful assembly and five others for "criminal provocation."

One of those arrested on the latter charge, a misdemeanor, was Mrs. Amelia Boynton, an insurance agent and local civil rights leader. When she refused to leave the sidewalk in front of the courthouse, Sheriff Clark grabbed her by the back of her collar and pushed her roughly and swiftly for half a block into a patrol car.

The Rev. Dr. Martin Luther King Jr. was watching from a car parked across the street. He stepped out of the car, walked into the Federal building, which faces the courthouse, and asked the Justice Department to file for a court injunction against the sheriff.

Dr. King, who is leading a voter registration drive throughout Alabama, charged that the arrests were unlawful and that the sheriff had been brutal. "I met with two officers of the Justice Department and filed a complaint that is to be immediately sent to Washington," he told reporters later. "It was one of the most brutal and unlawful acts I have seen an officer commit."

Dr. King left Selma tonight after telling a rally of 800 Negroes that he would return at the end of the week to continue "plaguing Dallas County — creatively and nonviolently."

PROJECT ANNOUNCED

He announced plans to set up a "freedom registration" project whereby a team of college professors would be brought in to draw up registration requirements they consider necessary to meet constitutional requirements.

"Negroes will go in and sign up by the thousands," he said, "and these will be presented to the Federal courts to show that discrimination exists."

Those arrested were released tonight pending arraignment without having to post bond.

Sheriff Clark, who has become a symbol of aggression to Selma Negroes, has been named a defendant in previous Justice Department suits, now pending in the courts. One charges that he used his office to prevent compliance with the public accommodations section of the Civil Rights Act of 1964.

Yesterday about 400 Negroes marched to the courthouse to register. Sheriff Clark directed them through the building and into an alley that had been cordoned off with ropes. They applicants stood there all day.

The courthouse was closed to reporters. But it was learned none of the Negroes took the written test prescribed by state law for registration. The registration board apparently used the day to test applicants already there when the Negroes arrived. When the group returned today, Sheriff Clark again assigned them to the alley. Normally, applicants wait in line in corridors and along the sidewalk. The lines form because only a few days in each month are set aside for registration.

When the Negroes refused to go into the alley today, Sheriff Clark arrested them for unlawful assembly. Those charged with criminal provocation were not trying to register, but they were leading the group.

In City Court, Jimmy George Robinson was fined $100 and sentenced to 60 days of hard labor for striking Dr. King in the lobby of the Hotel Albert yesterday. Robinson, 26 years old, of Birmingham, is a member of the National States Rights party, a small segregationist organization.

Judge Edgar P. Russell dismissed a charge of disorderly conduct against Robert A. Lloyd, 20, of Richmond, who was found in black face and costume in a restaurant about to be integrated. Lloyd, a member of the American Nazi party, said he had intended to mimic Negroes when they arrived to eat.

Dr. King, 300 Negroes Arrested in Selma

BY INTERNATIONAL HERALD TRIBUNE | FEB. 2, 1965

SELMA, ALA., FEB. 1 — Civil-rights leader the Rev. Martin Luther King Jr. was arrested today while attempting to lead a mass march of 300 Negroes on the Dallas county courthouse to protest voter-registration procedures. The Negroes, who were walking en masse from a church, were taken into custody on orders from Selma's Public Safety Director Wilson Baker on charges of parading without a permit. Mr. Baker stopped the procession near the church, where the Negroes had assembled. He told them: "Each and every one of you is under arrest for parading without a permit." After an hour of waiting in the jail, Dr. King was released without charges filed against him. But he was quickly rearrested when he did not obey an officer's orders to leave the scene. This was the first time he has been arrested since he received the Nobel Peace prize last month.

Freedom March Begins at Selma; Troops on Guard

BY ROY REED | MARCH 22, 1965

SELMA, ALA., MARCH 21 — Backed by the armed might of the United States, 3,200 persons marched out of Selma today on the first leg of a historic venture in nonviolent protest.

The marchers, or at least many of them, are on their way to the State Capitol at Montgomery to submit a petition for Negro rights Thursday to Gov. George C. Wallace, a man with little sympathy for their cause.

Today was the third attempt for the Alabama Freedom March. On the first two, the marchers were stopped by state troopers, the first time with tear gas and clubs.

The troopers were on hand today, but they limited themselves to helping Federal troops handle traffic on U.S. Highway 80 as the marchers left Selma.

SOLDIERS LINE HIGHWAY

Hundreds of Army and federalized National Guard troops stood guard in Selma and lined the highway out of town to protect the marchers. The troops were sent by President Johnson after Governor Wallace said that Alabama could not afford the expense of protecting the march.

The marchers were in festive humor as they started. The tone was set by the Rev. Ralph D. Abernathy, top aide to the Rev. Dr. Martin Luther King Jr. in the Southern Christian Leadership Conference, as he introduced Dr. King for an address before the march started.

"When we get to Montgomery," Mr. Abernathy said, "we are going to go up to Governor Wallace's door and say, 'George, it's all over now. We've got the ballot.' " The throng laughed and cheered.

ROBERT ABBOTT SENGSTACKE/GETTY IMAGES

The Rev. Dr. Martin Luther King Jr. and his wife, Coretta King, center, lead marchers from Selma to Montgomery, Ala. With them are the Rev. Ralph D. Abernathy, far left, and Dr. Ralph J. Bunche, third from left.

SEVEN MILES COVERED

The marchers, a large majority of them Negroes, walked a little over seven miles today.

Governor Wallace is not expected to be at the State Capitol when the marchers arrive at the end of their 54-mile journey. An aide has said that he will probably be "in Michigan, or someplace" making a speech Thursday.

Not enough buses could be found to escort 2,900 of the 3,200 marchers back to Selma tonight in line with a Federal Court order limiting the number to 300 along a two-lane stretch of highway.

The authorities feared for the safety of those returning to Selma. Justice Department officials finally arranged with the Southern Railway for a special train of the Western Railway of Alabama to take them back. The Western is a subsidiary of the Southern.

JOHNSON PRAISED

Highway 80 narrows from a four-lane to a two-lane road about five miles past the point where the marchers stopped tonight. It widens to four lanes again as it approaches Montgomery.

In his talk at the start of the march, Dr. King praised President Johnson, saying of his voting-rights message to Congress last Monday: "Never has a President spoken so eloquently or so sincerely on the question of civil rights."

Then he turned to the crowd in front of Browns Chapel Methodist Church, the thousands of whites and Negroes from Alabama and around the country who were congregated for the march, and said:

"You will be the people that will light a new chapter in the history books of our nation. Those of us who are Negroes don't have much. We have known the long night of poverty. Because of the system, we don't have much education and some of us don't know how to make our nouns and verbs agree. But thank God we have our bodies, our feet and our souls.

"Walk together, children, don't you get weary, and it will lead us to the promised land. And Alabama will be a new Alabama, and America will be a new America."

Dr. King's sense of history, if not his optimism, seemed well-placed. The Alabama march appears destined for a niche in the annals of the great protest demonstrations.

The march is the culmination of a turbulent nine-week campaign that began as an effort to abolish restrictions on Negro voting in the Alabama Black Belt and widened finally to encompass a general protest against racial injustice in the state.

The drive has left two men dead and scores injured. Some 3,800 persons have been arrested in Selma and neighboring communities.

The march got under way at 12:47 P.M., 2 hours 47 minutes late, after a confused flurry of last-minute planning and organizing.

The marchers reached the first night's campsite, 7.3 miles east of Selma, at 5:30. When they got there they found four big tents pitched in a Negro farmer's field.

Leading the march with Dr. King were Dr. Ralph J. Bunche, United Nations Under Secretary for Special Political Affairs; the Right Rev. Richard Millard, Suffragan Bishop of the Episcopal Diocese of California; and Cager Lee, grandfather of Jimmie Lee Jackson, the young Negro killed by a state trooper last month at Marion, Ala.

Also among the leaders were John Lewis, president of the Student Nonviolent Coordinating Committee; Deaconess Phyllis Edwards of the Episcopal Diocese of California; Rabbi Abraham Heschel, professor of Jewish mysticism and ethics at the Jewish Theological Seminary in New York; Mr. Abernathy, and the Rev. Frederick D. Reese, a Negro minister from Selma, who is president of the Dallas County Voters' League.

2,000 SPECTATORS

About 2,000 white and Negro spectators watched the procession leave town. That was 4,000 fewer than Army Intelligence had predicted.

About 150 whites watched in silence as the march turned from Alabama Avenue and headed down Broad Street toward Edmund Pettus Bridge. A white man hoisted his young son to his shoulder to give the lad a better view. Several persons snapped pictures.

Brig. Gen. Henry V. Graham, a National Guard officer, commanded all Federal troops on the scene, including the Regular Army military policemen. General Graham, a tall, square-jawed man, stood in the middle of Pettus Bridge wearing a helmet as he directed the operation.

Two state trooper cars led the procession across the bridge. In the lead car was Maj. John Cloud, the man who directed the rout, with tear gas and nightsticks, of 525 Negro marchers near the foot of the same bridge two weeks ago.

The marchers passed the site of the bloody incident without signal, except for a reminder from a white heckler.

It was to protest the officers' rout of the first marchers that the Rev. James J. Reeb, a white Unitarian minister from Boston, came to

Selma with scores of other clergymen. While he was here, Mr. Reeb was fatally beaten by a band of white men on March 9.

The heckler held up a sign as the procession left Pettus Bridge early this afternoon. It read, “Too bad, Reeb.”

A few feet away, another white spectator held a sign saying, “I hate niggers.”

MORE HECKLERS

More whites heckled from a railroad embankment running along the highway. They apparently were upset over the way the marchers were carrying a United States flag. They were carrying it upside down, the position of the distress signal.

On down the road, three cars painted with anti-Negro slogans passed in the south section of the four-lane highway. One car, with a Mississippi license plate, bore the words “Meridian, Miss., hates niggers.” A Confederate flag flew from the radio aerial. The lettering on another car said, “Go home scum.”

Back in town some 20 stragglers ran up Broad Street toward the bridge with knapsacks bouncing on their backs, trying to catch the procession, which had already disappeared over the bridge. The marchers walked on the left side of the highway.

The Federal presence was everywhere, even in the air. About a dozen planes and helicopters, many of them manned by military personnel, flew over the procession constantly.

John Doar, head of the Civil Rights Division of the Justice Department, walked to one side at the head of the march, watching.

Maj. Gen. Carl C. Turner, Provost Marshal General of the United States Army, was on the scene as the personal representative of the Army Chief of Staff, Gen. Harold K. Johnson.

By radio, Federal agents reported minute by minute to the Justice Department and the Pentagon in Washington.

M.P.s guarded every crossroad, leapfrogging in Jeeps to stay ahead of the march.

There was one report of violence. An unidentified white minister riding in an advance car was said to have been attacked by four white men when he got out of the car on the side of the road.

A spokesman for the marchers said the minister had been struck on the face once and knocked to the ground but had not been seriously hurt.

Today's leg of the journey was cut short four miles by a court injunction obtained by a white landowner who did not want the marchers camping overnight on his land. A Negro tenant had agreed to let them camp there.

The march leaders found a new campsite. The Negro farmer's field where they slept tonight is about a quarter of a mile south of the highway.

The field is about 500 yards from the New Sister Springs Baptist Church. It was at the church that the marchers returning to Selma tonight boarded rented Greyhound buses and numerous automobiles that shuttled them to the railway loading point about a mile from the campsite.

Most of those who left the march this way spent the night, as many had spent previous nights with Negro families in Selma.

Some will remain in Alabama, and rejoin the march Thursday, the final day. Leaders of the march hope to arrive at Montgomery in impressive numbers.

The military authorities are concerned about protection for the marchers at night. Show business personalities such as Harry Belafonte and Lena Horne are scheduled to entertain the group every night. The officials fear that outsiders may come to the camps to see and hear the entertainers, and that troublemakers may infiltrate at the same time.

A military spokesman said the troops had no authority to search cars for weapons.

Although the weather was relatively warm for the beginning of the march, the temperature dropped below freezing.

The coming of the troops to Selma has produced none of the crushing grimness of the Federal presence that characterized the Government's intervention at Little Rock, Ark., in 1957 and Oxford. Miss., in 1962.

The main difference is that troops were used in the earlier instances to suppress violence already out of hand, or threatening to get out of hand, while they were brought here to prevent violence.

Most of Selma's whites today went about their Sunday morning business, which is church, and only a few bothered with the commotion on Sylvan Street.

About 30 whites gathered at Broad Street and Alabama Avenue at midmorning to wait for the march to go by. The march was late, as expected, and while they waited, half a dozen spectators joshed with the four armed military policemen stationed there.

The state and local authorities have repeatedly urged Alabama whites to stay away from U.S. Highway 80 while the march is in progress.

Early this morning, two or three armed M.P.s were deployed at each intersection on the march route in the city. More were strung out along Highway 80 on the other side of Edmund Pettus Bridge. Several state troopers were scattered along the highway on the outskirts of the city.

At Craig Air Force Base, five miles east on Highway 80, a dozen big Army trucks could be seen from the road. They were filled with armed troops.

The temperature was 2 degrees above freezing when people began gathering in Sylvan Street this morning. The sun came out brilliantly, and by 11 A.M. the temperature was up to 42 degrees.

The marchers were out in everything from shirtsleeves to heavy coats. One elderly Negro wore a dress Air Force topcoat and a heavy wool headpiece that covered his head, throat and most of his face.

Paul R. Screvane, president of the New York City Council, showed up in a suit and blue overcoat. He and Mrs. Constance Baker Motley, Manhattan's Negro Borough President, joined the milling crowd in front of Browns Chapel at mid-morning.

Mr. Screvane explained why he was there.

"We came to represent Mayor Wagner and, we hope, the people of New York in what we consider to be a just cause," he said.

Dozens of union officials and clergymen came in today and joined the hundreds of ministers and students and civil rights workers already here.

A fresh college group arrived, 33 students and three professors from Canisius College, a Roman Catholic institution in Buffalo, N. Y. A sign thrust up from the group said, "Civil Man Wants Civil Rights."

Early today, plans for the march were still being hammered out. At 8 A.M., 400 or 500 persons milled in the street.

Milling has become the style of the movement in recent weeks, and the character of the milling has changed as hundreds of whites from the North, East and West have come into town to add their protest to the Negro's. The outsiders mill with a greater air of purpose.

The marchers who showed up very early today in front of Browns Chapel were from the hard core of the movement. Others did not begin to appear on Sylvan Street until the sun was high.

The Alabama Freedom March has a long history, as the leaders see it. The Rev. Andrew Young, executive assistant to Dr. King in the Southern Christian Leadership Conference, told reporters last night that the whole Alabama project went back to the Birmingham church bombing of 1963 in which five Negro children were killed.

"At that time," he said, "we began to ask ourselves, 'What can we do to change the climate of an entire state?' "

The Black Belt movement began that year. The Student Nonviolent Coordinating Committee moved into Selma, which calls itself queen of the Alabama Black Belt — the swath of rich, dark soil and heavy Negro population across south-central Alabama — and began holding meetings and demonstrations.

Dr. King and the Southern Christian Leadership Conference came here last January and put the Selma movement on the map.

Mass Integration Is Quiet in South

BY GENE ROBERTS | AUG. 31, 1965

ATLANTA, AUG. 30 — Thousands of Negro children quietly entered once-white schools in the South today as racial desegregation moved for the first time into many small cities and rural areas. Some educators said it was the biggest day of integration in the South's history.

While racial barriers were falling in the countryside, some of the South's cities shifted from token desegregation to massive integration.

No incidents of violence were reported, but some parents in Mississippi kept their children away from public schools and stepped up plans for private facilities.

By permitting desegregation, public school officials brought their school systems into compliance with the Civil Rights Act of 1964, and thus maintained their schools' eligibility for Federal aid.

The day was considered significant by civil rights leaders, not because of the total number of Negroes involved but because it marked the first time that many rural and small-city schools had opened their doors to Negro students.

Civil rights organizations look on much of today's desegregation as "token," but say it may double or triple last year's enrollment of 66,135 Negroes — or about 2.3 per cent of the South's school-age Negroes — in schools with white children.

Some Negroes entered previously all-white schools earlier this month. The principal influx started today, however, and will continue through the next two weeks, the period in which most of the region's schools open.

In many areas, school officials were reluctant to say how many Negroes had been enrolled for fear of possible segregationist resistance, but most agreed that the total would double or triple last year's desegregation figures.

In Atlanta, the day was a memorable one for the family of the Rev. Dr. Martin Luther King Jr., the Negro civil rights leader whose efforts to achieve peaceful integration won him the Nobel Peace Prize.

For the first time, Dr. King's children entered desegregated schools.

Martin Luther King 3d, 7 years old, and his sister, Yolanda, 9, along with three children of Dr. King's chief civil rights aide, Dr. Ralph Abernathy, became the first Negro children to enter Atlanta's Spring Street School under a "freedom of choice" plan adopted by Atlanta last year in anticipation of the civil rights legislation.

"Several parents welcomed us and said how happy they were to see us," Mrs. King said. "It went beautifully."

In Philadelphia, Miss., which became a symbol of hard-core resistance to desegregation a year ago when three civil rights workers were slain near there, nine students were admitted into white schools today without incident.

"It's just like we've been operating for years," said J. E. Hurdle, superintendent of Philadelphia's schools. And so it went through much of the South.

"We have schools opening in all sections of the city today — and many of them are integrated," said Austin Meadows, Alabama's school superintendent. "We've had no report of any incident."

A major factor in the absences of violence, some school officials said, is that most of the desegregation plans were shaped by local school boards with the support of "leading citizens."

Under the Civil Rights Act of 1964, the schools must either submit compliance plans or lose Federal aid. "Some people," said one school administrator, "felt they could fight the Supreme Court decision but think opposing a law of Congress is a different matter."

Federal Bureau of Investigation agents and 40 special sheriff's deputies appeared this morning at Hayneville School in Lowndes County, Ala., where five Negro children were expected to attend desegregated classes. The children did not appear, however.

Miss Hulda Coleman, the county school superintendent, said the parents of the children had agreed to enter them on the second rather than the first day of classes.

Among the deputies present at the Haynesville School were four Negroes, who were appointed by county officials as a "conciliatory gesture" nine days ago after a white seminarian was slain and another civil rights worker seriously wounded.

In Atlanta, School Superintendent John W. Letson estimated that between 2,000 and 2,500 Negro students attended school with white children in the Atlanta school system today, compared with 1,600 a year ago.

Other school spokesmen indicated that as many as 50 other schools throughout Georgia might have opened today on a desegregated basis, many of them in southwest Georgia, the area traditionally most opposed to racial integration.

At Lexington, Miss., on the edge of the Delta, 51 Negro students appeared at Durant School today for the first full day of classes, but all but six white students in the four desegregated classes — grades one through four — stayed home. School officials estimated that about 150 students participated in the boycott.

Meanwhile, many parents in Lexington and adjoining areas of Holmes County moved ahead with plans for a private school. They announced that the First Baptist Church in Lexington had agreed to make its facilities available. Private schools were also under consideration in other areas of the state.

In Charlotte, N.C., over 2,000 Negroes reported for desegregated classes today — two-thirds as many as the entire state admitted on a desegregated basis last year. In two of the state's tobacco belt counties, Wilson and Harnett — desegregation spread out of the towns and cities into the rural areas for the first time.

There was tension but no violence in coastal North Carolina, where concentrations of state policemen and investigative agents gathered to protect Negroes attending Craven County schools. Gov. Dan Moore dispatched the law enforcement officers to New Bern, Craven's county seat, last week after parents of some of the children said they had received threatening phone calls.

School attendance was light in Louisiana, where the state was observing the birthday of former Governor and Senator Huey Long, who was slain by an assassin's bullet more than a quarter of a century ago. Desegregation was scheduled to take place there later this week, however, in at least 18 school districts and dozens of individual schools. The State School Board Association estimated today that 1,750 Negro pupils had been admitted to once-white schools in the state.

South Carolina, which admitted 800 Negroes to predominantly white schools last week, admitted still more today. The total was expected to grow to more than 2,000 early next week.

A spokesman for the United States Office of Education in Washington said that it had approved desegregation plans submitted by 1,444 school districts in 17 Southern and border states. Forty more have been accepted pending ratification by local school boards and 151 have been "agreed upon in principle."

The spokesman said 153 districts had submitted incomplete compliance plans and another 153 would require extensive negotiations "as they fall far below acceptable standards."

At least 149 school districts have not yet prepared compliance plans and will presumably turn away any Negroes who might apply for admission, the spokesman said.

The school system in Sumter County, Ga., a racial battleground during much of this summer, is among those that have not submitted a plan. It has thus put in jeopardy $171,596 it hoped to receive in Federal aid this year. The school system in Americus, Sumter's county seat, has registered 87 Negroes. Most of them appeared for classes today.

Other schools in areas that have become symbolic of the South's resistance to desegregation, are moving ahead with desegregation plans.

The Drew School in Sunflower County, Miss., announced today it planned to admit Negroes Sept. 6 into previously all-white classes.

CHAPTER 3

A Conflicted Civil Rights Movement

Although there were significant civil rights gains under Dr. King's leadership, support for the movement — and for passive resistance — began to wane. Factions supporting "black power" and the separation of blacks and whites rose in profile. The federal government was focused on its military involvement in Vietnam, a war that Dr. King vociferously opposed. He claimed it was depleting resources from the fight against racial discrimination in the United States. His position was controversial, and many believed it was a mistake to link civil rights with the antiwar protests.

Civil Rights and War

BY JOHN HERBERS | AUG. 5, 1965

WASHINGTON, JULY 4 — The Negro revolution, which has been concerned primarily with attacking racial discrimination, is showing signs as well of becoming a vehicle for opposition to the United States military posture abroad. Although there has traditionally been a close relationship between the civil rights and peace movements, most Negro leaders have avoided issues of foreign policy for tactical reasons.

Chief among these leaders has been the Rev. Dr. Martin Luther King Jr., president of the Southern Christian Leadership Conference. Last week Dr. King told an audience of Negro leaders in Petersburg,

Va., that the time had come for the civil rights movement to become involved with the problem of war.

'THE LONG NIGHT'

"It is worthless," he said, "to talk about integrating if there is no world to integrate in." He went on: "I certainly am as concerned about seeing the defeat of Communism as anyone else, but we won't defeat Communism by guns or bombs or gases. We will do it by making democracy work.

"The war in Vietnam must be stopped. There must be a negotiated settlement even with the Vietcong. The long night of war must be stopped."

To those accustomed to hearing Dr. King speak, the words had a strange sound. Suddenly the imagery of "the long night," which Dr. King has used to describe the plight of the American Negro, had been shifted to Southeast Asia.

After the speech, Dr. King said in response to questions that the directors of his Atlanta-based organization had discussed the possibility of holding "peace rallies just like we have freedom rallies." He said they might be similar to the campus teach-ins held by critics of American policy in Vietnam.

WILKINS VOICES DOUBT

Some other Negro leaders, however, have reservations about civil rights organizations taking any position on foreign policy. Roy Wilkins, the executive director of the National Association for the Advancement of Colored People, said today, "We have enough Vietnams in Alabama."

Mr. Wilkins was interviewed on the C.B.S. radio and television program "Face the Nation." He said:

"When you mix the question of Vietnam into the questions of Mississippi and Alabama and getting registration and the vote and all the things that the American Negroes want in this country, you sort of confuse the issue."

After the program Mr. Wilkins said, "The American Negro can be of greater aid to foreign policy and other problems as he grows stronger

ROBERT ABBOTT SENGSTACKE/GETTY IMAGES

The Rev. Dr. Martin Luther King Jr. speaking at a rally in Chicago, Ill.

in this country. His first thought ought to be to strengthen his position as an American. If he's a third-rate citizen his opinions on South Africa or Vietnam will have no effect."

While the major civil rights organizations have refrained from becoming formally committed to the peace movement, their leaders' increased participation in it is seen as opening up the possibility of a new force against American military involvement abroad.

The decision to broaden the Negro protest is part of the new direction the civil rights movement has taken now that most legal barriers to equality have been removed. The trend is to put less emphasis on direct action against racial discrimination and more on politically activating the poor and underprivileged.

A few days ago the Fellowship of Reconciliation, a peace group based in New York, held a conference on the campus of Georgetown University here to explore the possibility of a merger between the peace and civil rights movements.

FARMER'S VIEW

One of the speakers was James Farmer, national director of the Congress of Racial Equality. A woman in the audience who had spent many hours picketing the White House said, "As if the Pentagon was not enough, I understand a new Defense Building is to be constructed in Washington. Now here is an opportunity for the peace and civil rights movements to get together in protest."

Mr. Farmer said that he would approve of such action "on an ad hoc basis," but that he did not believe there should be any formal merger of the two movements.

"CORE should not be a peace movement," he said. "It would divert too much of our energies. Yet on specific issues the two should be coordinated. As an individual I object to our Vietnam policies. As individuals we should and would be involved in both."

Mr. Farmer said most Negro leaders believed that much of the military budget should be diverted to domestic projects such as the eradication of poverty and slums.

The Rev. Andrew Young, one of Dr. King's chief assistants, said in a telephone interview that the Southern Christian Leadership Conference "is not about to switch purposes."

Many supporters of civil rights also support the Johnson Administration's foreign policy, Mr. Young noted. He added, however, that most Negro leaders, particularly those who have adopted nonviolence as "a way of life," had an affinity for the peace movement.

Negroes, he said, have the feeling that much of American foreign policy is based on a prejudice against dark-skinned people.

"One day during the Dominican crisis," Mr. Young said, "we were looking at television and my young son asked me. 'Daddy, why are the marines shooting at the colored people?' "

"After all," Mr. Young said, "the purpose of our voting rights is specifically to get rid of people like Russell."

He referred to Senator Richard B. Russell, Democrat of Georgia, who has opposed civil rights legislation. As chairman of the Senate

Armed Services Committee, Senator Russell has followed a hard line on foreign policy.

In both the civil rights and peace movements, there has been a proliferation of organizations representing a wide spectrum of opinion. Peace groups range from those opposing any military action or use of force to those seeking gradual disarmament.

Some of the civil rights organizations have pacifist roots. CORE was an outgrowth of the Fellowship of Reconciliation. Dr. King and others adopted the nonviolent tactics of Gandhi. Many pacifist leaders have been active in civil rights, and vice versa.

In 1963 the Committee for Nonviolent Action, a pacifist group based in Connecticut, staged a peace march from Quebec to Havana. The marchers were a mixture of pacifists and civil rights workers who had served time in Southern jails as a result of their protests against segregation.

Last April, 15,000 students picketed the White House demanding an end to the fighting in Vietnam. The Student Nonviolent Coordinating Committee a civil rights organization based in Atlanta, was one of the sponsors of the protest.

At the conference sponsored here by the Fellowship of Reconciliation, Norman Thomas, the former Socialist candidate for President, was asked about the possibility of forming a political party through a coalition of civil rights and peace groups.

"It would be very difficult," he said. "They can get together to dissent but when it comes to practical politics, that does not work. I remember people [in the civil rights movement] used to tell us, 'We can't take a chance on being a Socialist as well as a Negro — one is enough.' "

Dr. King Advocates Quitting Vietnam

BY GLADWIN HILL | FEB. 26, 1967

BEVERLY HILLS, CALIF., FEB. 25 — Four Senators joined the Rev. Dr. Martin Luther King Jr., Negro civil rights leader, as leading participants today in a conference whose theme was United States withdrawal from the Vietnam conflict.

Dr. King asserted that the United States' involvement had violated the United Nations Charter and the principle of self-determination had crippled the antipoverty program and had impaired the right of dissent.

The Senators were Eugene J. McCarthy of Minnesota, George S. McGovern of South Lakota and Ernest Gruening of Alaska, Democrats, and Mark O. Hatfield of Oregon, a Republican.

The conference, entitled "National Priority No. 1: Redirecting American Power" was conducted by The Nation magazine with headquarters in New York. An overflow audience of 1,500 persons attended the all-day meeting at the Beverly Hilton Hotel.

The magazine's publisher, James J. Storrow Jr., said the conference was held in California because the state "is at once the most liberal and the most conservative, sensitive to foreign policy, quicker to sense changes in the Far East than the rest of the nation and because Californians take bold initiatives."

In the meeting's main address, at a luncheon, Dr. King, who heads the Southern Christian Leadership Conference, contended that the United States' failure to submit its case against the North Vietnamese to the United Nations Security Council had "undermined the purpose of the U.N., caused its effectiveness to atrophy and placed our nation in the position of being morally and politically isolated."

The United States activities in Vietnam, he said, amounted to "supporting a new form of colonialism covered up by certain niceties of complexity."

NOBEL PRIZE WINNER

As a result of President Truman's feeling "that the Vietnamese people were not ready for independence," the Atlanta minister who won the Nobel Peace Prize in 1964 said, "for nine years we supported the French in their abortive effort to recolonize Vietnam." United States Government officials began to brainwash the American public. We supported Ngo Dinh Diem in his betrayal of the Geneva accord," he continued, leaving this country "in an untenable position morally and politically."

"The promises of the Great Society have been shot down on the battlefield of Vietnam," Dr. King continued.

"The pursuit of this widened war has narrowed domestic welfare programs, making the poor, white and Negro, bear the heaviest burdens both at the front and at home. The recently revealed $10-billion mis-estimate of the war budget alone is more than five times the amount committed to antipoverty programs. The security we profess to seek in foreign adventures we will lose in our decaying cities.

"We are willing to make the Negro 100 per cent of a citizen in warfare, but reduce him to 50 per cent of a citizen on American soil. Half of all Negroes live in substandard housing and he has half the income of whites. There is twice as much unemployment and infant mortality among Negroes. There were twice as many Negroes in combat in Vietnam at the beginning of 1967 and twice as many died in action — 20.6 per cent — in proportion to their numbers in the population as whites."

CALL TO CONSCIENCE

"We are presently moving down a dead-end road that can lead to national disaster. It is time for all people of conscience to call upon America to return to her true home of brotherhood and peaceful pursuits. Those of us who love peace must organize as effectively as the war hawks."

Remarking that he agreed with Henry Steele Commager, the historian, who told a Senate committee this week that the United States was trying to do too much towards stabilizing the world, Dr. King concluded:

"There is an element of urgency in our redirecting of American power. We still have a choice: nonviolent coexistence, or violent co-annihilation. It is still not too late to make the proper choice."

Senator McCarthy said:

"We should hesitate to waste our strength — economic, military and moral — in so highly a questionable a course. We must not do the wrong things for the right reasons."

Senator Hatfield, elected last November as a leading critic of the country's Vietnam commitment, questioned the wisdom of the manpower and money involved in the Vietnam war and suggested:

"We must reorder our priorities. We must rationally decide if our goal of preserving liberty is better served through huge expenditures to beat the Russians — or through developing methods to feed a hungry world."

Senator McGovern, focusing on the United States' position vis-à-vis Communist China, asserted:

"We have neither the mission nor the capacity to play God in Asia by a unilateral United States police operation."

Dr. King Will Join a Vietnam Protest On April 15 at U.N.

BY THE NEW YORK TIMES | MARCH 17, 1967

THE REV. MARTIN LUTHER KING JR. has agreed to play a leading role in an antiwar demonstration scheduled to be held here on April 15 outside United Nations headquarters.

The civil rights leader, who has been increasingly critical in recent months of the United States role in Vietnam, will participate in a march from Central Park to the United Nations and will then address a rally.

Dr. King's decision to join the demonstration was announced yesterday by leaders of the Spring Mobilization to End the war in Vietnam, an amalgam of peace groups that is sponsoring similar protests on April 15 in New York and San Francisco.

The Rev. James Bevel, who is on leave from Dr. King's Southern Christian leadership Conference to organize the protests, said that the Negro leader's presence would "symbolize the growing awareness in black communities that this is a racist war."

Mr. Bevel disclosed Dr. King's role at a news conference at the Overseas Press Club. He said that Floyd B. McKissick, national director of the Congress of Racial Equality, would participate in the San Francisco protest.

Among those attending the news conference was Robert Greenblatt, an assistant professor of mathematics at Cornell University who is a member of the Interuniversity Committee for Debate on Foreign Policy, and Dr. Benjamin Spock, the noted pediatrician, who is chairman of the New York rally.

Dr. King to Weigh Civil Disobedience If War Intensifies

BY THE NEW YORK TIMES | APRIL 2, 1967

LOUISVILLE, KY., MARCH 30 — The Rev. Dr. Martin Luther King Jr. said today that if the United States continued to step up the war in Vietnam, civil disobedience might be necessary as a form of protest.

The civil rights leader emphasized that he was not advocating civil disobedience at this time. But he said, "If our nation insists on escalating the war and if we don't see any changes, it may be necessary to engage in civil disobedience to further arouse the conscience of the nation and make it clear we feel this is hurting our country."

He expressed these and other views in a recorded interview with John Herbers of The New York Times while attending a two-day conference of the board of directors of the Southern Christian Leadership Conference, which he heads, in the Zion Baptist Church.

Following are questions and answers from the interview:

Q. *Dr. King, in recent days you have become increasingly outspoken against the war in Vietnam. Why the increased opposition at this particular time?*

A. Well, I would say there are at least three reasons why I felt compelled to take a stronger stand against the war in Vietnam. First, I feel this war is playing havoc with our domestic destinies. As long as the war in Vietnam goes on, the more difficult it will be to implement the programs that will deal with the economic and social problems that Negro people confront in our country and poor people generally.

So in a real sense, the Great Society has been shot down on the battlefield of Vietnam. I feel it is necessary to take a stand against it or at least arouse the conscience of the nation against it so that at least we can move more and more toward a negotiated settlement of that terrible conflict.

There is another reason why I feel compelled at this time to take a stand against the war and that is that the constant escalation of the war in Vietnam can lead to a grand war with China and to a kind of full world war that could mean the annihilation of the human race.

And I think those of us who are concerned about the survival of mankind, those of us who feel and know that mankind should survive must take a stand against this war because it is more than just a local conflict on Asian soil. It is a conflict that in a real sense affects the whole world and makes possible, at least brings into being the possibility of, the destruction of all mankind, so because of my concerns for mankind and the survival of mankind, I feel the need to take a stand.

The other reason is I have preached nonviolence in the movement in our country, and I think it is very consistent for me to follow a nonviolent approach in international affairs. It would be very inconsistent for me to teach and preach nonviolence in this situation and then applaud violence when thousands and thousands of people, both adults and children, are being maimed and mutilated and many killed in this war, so that I still feel and live by the principle, "Thou shalt not kill."

And it is out of this moral commitment to dignity and the worth of human personality that I feel it is necessary to stand up against the war in Vietnam.

RIGHTS DRIVE MIGRATION

Q. *In 1965, there was an influx of civil rights workers, mostly those identified with the more radical groups such as the Student Nonviolence Coordinating Committee, into the peace movement. At that time I believe you condemned the war but kept your organization and energies pretty well channeled in the civil rights movement.*

Recently , one of your assistants, the Rev. James Bevel, moved full time into the peace movement and is now organizing a protest in New York April 15 in which he will participate. Do you foresee a mass migration from civil rights to the peace movement?

A. No, I don't think there will be a mass migration from the civil rights movement if by that you mean leaving civil rights. I think more and more of them will become involved in both kinds of programmatic action.

There are many Negroes who now feel the two problems, the two issues, are inextricably bound together and that you can't really have freedom without justice, you can't have peace without justice, and you can't have justice without peace, so it is more of a realization of the interrelatedness of racism and militarism and the need to attack both problems rather than leaving one.

Certainly we will continue to work in both areas, but I feel, and many others that I have talked to agree, that we are merely marking time in the civil rights movement if we do not take a stand against the war. The fact is that while it may be true technically and from a monetary point of view that you can have guns and butter, it is a fact of life that where your heart is there your money will go, and the heart of the Administration is in that war in Vietnam.

The heart of the Congress is in the war. As long as that is true, that is where the money will go, and I feel that we are in need of a radical reorientation of our national priorities. This war is keeping us to the point where we aren't really reordering things.

Q. *If the war continues and worsens despite peaceful demonstrations against it in this country, do you think the peace movement should engage in civil disobedience of the kind the civil rights movement has used with some success in the past?*

A. I have not yet gone that far. But I wouldn't say it won't be necessary. It depends on developments over the next few months. I feel like the United States must take the first steps, I mean the initiative, to create an atmosphere for negotiations. We are so much more powerful than Vietnam.

We are the greatest military power and we don't need to prove our military power. I think we are superbly well placed, equipped to take the initiative in this and create the atmosphere for negotiations by ceasing bombings and some of the other things we are doing. Now if our nation insists on escalating the war and if we don't see any changes it may be necessary to engage in civil disobedience to further arouse the conscience of the nation and make it clear we feel this is hurting our country

And I might say this is another basic reason why I am involved and concerned. It is because I love America. I am not engaged in a hate American campaign. I would hope that the people of this country standing up against the war are standing up against it because they love America and because they want to see our great nation really stand up as the moral example of the world.

The fact is we have alienated ourselves from so much of the world and have become morally and politically isolated as the result of our involvement in the war in Vietnam.

PEACE DEMONSTRATIONS

Q. *Do you think civil rights organizations as such should join in peace demonstrations?*

A. I would certainly say that individuals in the civil rights movement should join in peace demonstrations. I have to make a distinction at this point because of my own involvement, and that is I made a decision to become involved as an individual, as a clergyman, as one who is greatly concerned about peace.

S.C.L.C. as an organization has not yet become actively involved in the peace movement. There are many individuals in S.C.L.C. who are involved, but organizationally S.C.L.C. has backed me in all the decisions I have made and all the stands I have taken without becoming a peace organization.

Now this may be the way it will have to continue, but civil rights organizations will continue engaging in purely civil rights activities, leaving the way open for persons on staffs and persons on boards, and what have you, and the membership can, as individuals, feel free to participate.

I do feel that organizationally we are limited in terms of resources and energies in what we can do, and this means we probably will have to continue to give our prime time and work to civil rights activities through the civil rights organizations. But I as an individual will continue to stand up on the issue of peace and against the war in Vietnam.

Q. *Dr. King, I understand you have been away for some time writing a new book and contemplating where to go from here. Did you reach any conclusions on where the civil rights movement is headed?*

A. Well, I reached several conclusions which will be stated in the book. One of the things I tried to state in the first chapter is that for more than a decade we worked mainly to remove the stigma and humiliation of legal segregation. We have made some significant victories in this area. Many people in the nation, whites, joined in taking a stand against this kind of humiliation of the Negro.

But what we are faced with now is the fact that the struggle must be and actually is at this point a struggle for genuine equality. The struggle over the last 10 or 12 years has been a struggle for decency, a struggle to get rid of extremist behavior towards Negroes, and I think we are moving in to a period which is much more difficult because it is dealing with hard economic problems which will cost the nation something to solve.

It did not cost the nation anything to integrate lunch counters or public accommodations. It did not cost the nation anything to guarantee the right to vote. The problem now is in order — to end the long night of poverty and economic insecurity — it would mean billions of dollars. In order to get rid of bad education, education devoid of poverty, it means lifting the educational level of the whole public school system, which would mean billions of dollars.

This, I feel, is much more difficult than the period we have gone through. There will be more resistance because it means the privileged groups will have to give up some of their billions. And I think the so-called white backlash is expressed right here.

It is a reaction to the demands that are presently being made by Negroes now demanding genuine equality, and not just integration of the lunch counters but an adequate wage; not just integration of the classrooms, but a decent sanitary house in which to live. It is much easier to integrate a restaurant than it is to demand an annual income. I think the growing debate is recognition of this difficulty.

The next conclusion I reached is that the great need in the Negro community and the civil rights movement is to organize the Negro community for the amassing of real political and economic power. The questions now is not merely developing programs because we have put many programs on paper.

What is needed now is the undergirding power to bring about enough pressure so that these programs can become a reality, that they can become concretized in our everyday lives; not only under the legislative process but under all the processes necessary to make them real. This just means the hard job of organizing tenants, organizing welfare recipients, organizing the unemployed and the underemployed.

It is for this reason that I am recommending to the Southern Christian Leadership Conference that we begin to train more field organizers so that we can really go out and organize these people and thereby move into the area of political action. I think the Negro can improve his economic resources much more if these resources are pooled, and I intend to do much more in this area so that we can make an economic thrust.

Q. *Dr. King, you have been called to the White House on many occasions to confer with the President about civil rights matters. Has your opposition to the war altered your relations in any way with President Johnson?*

A. Not as far as I am concerned. I go to the White House when he invites me. I have followed a policy of being very honest with the President when he has consulted me about civil rights.

I have made it very clear to him why I have taken a stand against the war in Vietnam. I had a long talk with him on the telephone not too many months ago about this and made it clear to him I would be standing up against it even more. I am not centering this on President Johnson. I think there is collective guilt.

CIVIL RIGHTS BILLS

Four presidents participated in some way leading us to the war in Vietnam. So I am not going to put it all on President Johnson. What I am concerned about now is that we end this nightmarish war and free our souls. I think that our souls are so terribly scarred now that as long as we are involved they get scarred more.

I will continue to be concerned, and if the President invites me to the White House on civil rights I will respond to it.

Q. *What about the President's civil rights bill now before Congress? Are they relevant to today's problems?*

A. They are all relevant to today's problems, but they are not adequate. One aspect of the inadequacy is the failure to call for immediacy.

The housing problem, I believe, is one of the greatest problems facing our nation. There is no more dangerous trend than the constant growth of predominantly Negro central cities ringed by white suburbs. I think this is only inviting social disaster.

I don't see any answer to it but an open housing law that is vigorously enforced. The Administration's bill does not call this year for a housing bill that is immediately enforceable. It would take three years to become nationally and universally applicable.

I don't think that is recognition of the urgency, and there is so much urgency about it that the more we stall on it the more the ghetto intensifies, the more the frustrations of the ghetto will intensify, so I don't think it is adequate because it does not call for immediate implementation.

The legislation on the administration of justice is necessary and relevant because we know that in the South Negroes and white civil rights workers are still being murdered and brutalized at whim, and trampled over at will and a lot of this happens because they think they can get by with it, because they feel they are aided and abetted by the law enforcement agencies in those particular areas.

Q. *What in your opinion is the current state of race relations in this country? Have there been gains? Do you still have hope?*

A. We have certainly made some gains. The greatest gain is that we have brought the issue out into the open so that nobody can escape it, nobody can say there isn't a race problem.

For years, many people deluded themselves and argued that the Negro was satisfied, that conditions were well. But now everybody knows that things aren't right and the Negro is not satisfied. We have exposed the injustices and brought the evils out into the open. This is probably the greatest achievement.

The other is a psychological achievement and many people overlook this, and that is the new sense of dignity, the new sense of manhood within the Negro himself. And I think this is probably the greatest victory, that the Negro has a new sense of dignity, a new sense of destiny, a new sense of self-respect as the result of the struggle over the last few years.

Also, we have made very significant legislative strides. The Civil Rights Bill of 1964 represented progress; the Voting Rights Bill of 1965 represented real progress. The problem is that these particular gains are legislative victories that did very little to rectify conditions facing millions of Negroes in the teeming ghettos of the North.

The rectified wrongs and evils in the South, but did very little to penetrate the lower depths of Negro deprivation in the North. Consequently, we do not see worse slums today in many parts. The schools in the North are more segregated today than they were in 1954. And, as I said earlier, the Negroes' economic problem is at many points worse today because of Negro unemployment and growing gulfs between white and Negro income.

Now this tells us that we still have a long way to go. But I'm not one to lose faith in the future or lose hope because I think the minute you do that you defeat the force that makes a revolution powerful. A revolution cannot survive on despair. It always must move on a wave of rising expectations and the feeling that you can win.

The minute you begin to feel that you can't win, you begin to adopt a no-win policy and to develop a nihilistic approach. I refuse to engage in that kind of hopelessness.

I still believe that we have in this country forces of goodwill that can be mobilized and that can direct the condition of conscience that will finally bring about this day when racism is no longer at the center of our society.

Dr. King Proposes a Boycott Of War

BY DOUGLAS ROBINSON | APRIL 5, 1967

THE REV. DR. MARTIN LUTHER KING JR. called yesterday on Negroes and "all white people of good will" to boycott the Vietnam war by becoming conscientious objectors to military service.

The civil rights leader, in making his strongest recommendations so far, said at a news conference that "Negroes and poor people generally are bearing the heaviest burden of this war."

Later, in a speech to an overflow crowd of more than 3,000 people at Riverside Church, Dr. King described the American Government as the "greatest purveyor of violence in the world today." His address was enthusiastically greeted by the throng, which gave him a standing ovation at the beginning and end of his talk.

OFFERS FIVE-POINT PLAN

He also laid out a five-point program designed to "begin the long and difficult process of extricating ourselves from this nightmarish conflict."

In his address, which was sponsored by the Clergy and Laymen Concerned About Vietnam, Dr. King likened the use of new American weapons on the peasants of Vietnam to the Germans' testing of "new medicine and new tortures in the concentration camps of Europe."

"If America's soul becomes totally poisoned, part of the autopsy must read Vietnam," Dr. King said.

Dr. King first made the recommendation for a program of conscientious objection at an early morning news conference at the Overseas Press Club, after noting that Negroes were "dying in disproportionate numbers in Vietnam."

"Twice as many Negroes as whites are in combat," he said, adding that this was a "reflection of the Negro's position in America."

In recommending avoidance of military service by those who are against the war, he said he would encourage all clergymen of draft age to give up their ministerial exemptions and seek status as conscientious objectors.

Dr. King also urged a campaign of teach-ins and preach-ins to "awaken the conscience of the nation" to what he termed the evils of the Vietnam conflict.

Later, in his speech at Riverside Church, Dr. King said he recommended conscientious objection "to all who find the American course in Vietnam a dishonorable and unjust one."

URGES U.S. ATONEMENT

In suggesting his program, Dr. King said that "in order to atone for our sins and errors in Vietnam, we should take the initiative in bringing a halt to this tragic war."

His program was as follows:

• The end of all bombing in North and South Vietnam.

• The declaration of a unilateral cease-fire in the hope that such action would create an atmosphere for negotiation.

• The taking of immediate steps to prevent other wars from developing in Southeast Asia by curtailing the military buildup in Thailand and interference in Laos.

• The recognition that the National Liberation Front has substantial support in South Vietnam and must therefore play a role in any meaningful negotiations and in any future Vietnam Government.

• The establishment of a date on which the United States will remove all foreign troops from Vietnam in accordance with the Geneva Agreement of 1954.

The agreement, which ended the French Indochina war, created a demarcation line across Vietnam at the 17th parallel and provided for the eventual unification of the nation through elections, which were never held.

URGES OFFER OF ASYLUM

Dr. King said that "part of our ongoing commitment might well express itself in an offer to grant asylum to any Vietnamese who fears for his life under a new regime which included the Liberation Front."

In tracing the course of American involvement in Vietnam, the civil rights leader suggested that this country was on the wrong side of a world revolution and urged that United States leaders admit "that we have been wrong from the beginning of our adventure in Vietnam."

Dr. King bitterly assailed American military policy from the standpoint of the Vietnamese peasants who "watch as we poison their water, as we kill a million acres of their crops."

"They must weep as the bulldozers roar through their areas preparing to destroy the precious trees," he said. "They wander into the hospitals, with at least 20 casualties from American firepower for one Vietcong-inflicted injury."

"So far, we may have killed a million of them — mostly children," he went on. "They wander into the towns and see thousands of the children, homeless, without clothes, running in packs on the streets like animals. They see the children degraded by our soldiers as they beg for food. They see the children selling their sisters to our soldiers, soliciting for their mothers."

In summing up, Dr. King said that "a nation that continues year after year to spend more money on military defense than on programs of social uplift is approaching spiritual death."

Sharing the platform with Dr. King was Dr. Henry Steele Commager, the historian, who described the Vietnam war as the "product of a body of political and historical miscalculation and of moral and psychological obsessions."

"It is the product of an obsession with Communism — we call it a conspiracy just as the Communists used to talk about capitalist conspiracies — something that is, therefore, not nearly a rival political or economic system, but an irradicable moral evil," Dr. Commager said.

Outside the church, at 122d Street and Riverside Drive, some 35 picketers marched and chanted in protest against Dr. King's stand. Some of the protesters were black nationalists. Others belonged to a group called the National Economic Growth and Reconstruction Organization (N.E.G.R.O.).

The leader of the organization, Dr. Herbert I. Mathew, who is director of the Interfaith Hospital in Queens, said he did not want to picket Dr. King but that "bigots were looking for issues to harm the civil rights movement."

"The patriotism of Negroes should never be questioned," Dr. Mathew said. "Dr. King is not speaking for all Negroes."

The Clergy and Laymen Concerned About Vietnam, the sponsoring organization, was formed in 1966 and says it has 5,000 to 6,000 members throughout the nation. The biracial interfaith group has urged the United States Government to cease bombing North Vietnam and to reduce the fighting in South Vietnam to create a climate for peace talks to end the Vietnam war as quickly as possible.

Dr. King's Error

BY THE NEW YORK TIMES | APRIL 7, 1967

IN RECENT speeches and statements the Rev. Dr. Martin Luther King Jr. has linked his personal opposition to the war in Vietnam with the cause of Negro equality in the United States. The war, he argues, should be stopped not only because it is a futile war waged for the wrong ends but also because it is a barrier to social progress in this country and therefore prevents Negroes from achieving their just place in American life.

This is a fusing of two public problems that are distinct and separate. By drawing them together, Dr. King has done a disservice to both. The moral issues in Vietnam are less clear-cut than he suggests the political strategy of uniting the peace movement and the civil rights movement could very well be disastrous for both causes.

Because American Negroes are a minority and have to overcome unique handicaps of racial antipathy and prolonged deprivation, they have a hard time in gaining their objectives even when their grievances are self-evident and their claims are indisputably just. As Dr. King knows from the Montgomery bus boycott and other civil rights struggles of the past dozen years, it takes almost infinite patience, persistence and courage to achieve the relatively simple aims that ought to be theirs by right.

The movement toward racial equality is now in the more advanced and more difficult stage of fulfilling basic rights by finding more jobs, changing patterns of housing and upgrading education. The battlegrounds in this struggle are Chicago and Harlem and Watts. The Negroes on these fronts need all the leadership, dedication and moral inspiration that they can summon and under these circumstances to divert the energies of the civil rights movement to the Vietnam issue is both wasteful and self-defeating.

Dr. King makes too facile a connection between the speeding up of the war in Vietnam and the slowing down of the war against poverty.

The eradication of poverty is at best the task of a generation. This "war" inevitably meets diverse resistance such as the hostility of local political machines, the skepticism of conservatives in Congress and the intractability of slum mores and habits. The nation could afford to make more funds available to combat poverty even while the war in Vietnam continues, but there is no certainty that the coming of peace would automatically lead to a sharp increase in funds.

Furthermore, Dr. King can only antagonize opinion in this country instead of winning recruits to the peace movement by recklessly comparing American military methods to those of the Nazis testing "new medicine and new tortures in the concentration camps of Europe." The facts are harsh, but they do not justify such slander. Furthermore, it is possible to disagree with many aspects of United States policy in Vietnam without whitewashing Hanoi.

As an individual, Dr. King has the right and even the moral obligation to explore the ethical implications of the war in Vietnam, but as one of the most respected leaders of the civil rights movement he has an equally weighty obligation to direct that movement's efforts in the most constructive and relevant way.

There are no simple or easy answers to the war in Vietnam or to racial injustice in this country. Linking these hard, complex problems will lead not to solutions but to deeper confusion.

N.A.A.C.P. Decries Stand Of Dr. King on Vietnam

BY THE NEW YORK TIMES | APRIL 11, 1967

THE DIRECTORS OF the National Association for the Advancement of Colored People voted unanimously yesterday against the proposal by the Rev. Dr. Martin Luther King Jr. to merge the civil rights and peace movements.

The 60-member board called Dr. King's plan "a serious tactical mistake." In a resolution adopted at its quarterly meeting here, the board said the effort to fuse the two movements "will serve the cause neither of civil rights nor of peace."

Dr. King, in a speech here last Tuesday, called on Negroes and "all whites of goodwill" to boycott the Vietnam war by becoming conscientious objectors to military service.

"A nation that continues year after year to spend more money on military defense than on programs of social uplift is approaching spiritual death," Dr. King had asserted.

The resolution adopted by the N.A.A.C.P. declared:

"Civil rights battles will have to be fought and won on their own merits, irrespective of the state of war or peace in the world.

"We are not a peace organization nor a foreign policy association. We are a civil rights organization. The N.A.A.C.P. remains committed to its primary goal of eliminating all forms of racial discrimination and achieving equal rights and equal opportunities for all Americans.

"We are, of course, for a just peace. But there already exist dedicated organizations whose No. 1 task is to work for peace just as our No. 1 job is to work for civil rights."

The statement, which did not mention Dr. King by name, was the first by the group on the war in Vietnam. Last week Whitney M. Young Jr., director of the National Urban League, said the peace and civil rights movements had different goals and that it would be inappropriate to merge them.

TIME FOR DECLARATION

The N.A.A.C.P.'s director of public relations, Henry Lee Moon, asked whether the resolution had been intended as a reply to Dr. King, said:

"We felt it was time to make a declaration, to make our position clear."

Dr. King's speech also drew criticism yesterday from Senator Jacob K. Javits, Republican of New York:

"It's certainly bound to be resented," Senator Javits said, "by the country which is deeply involved in the war and which feels it can certainly do justice by the Negro at one and the same time."

Dr. King could not be reached for comment.

In his speech, Dr. King had charged that "Negroes and poor people generally are bearing the heaviest burden of this war" and described the United States Government as the "greatest purveyor of violence in the world today."

He had likened the use of new American weapons in Vietnam to the Germans' testing of "new medicine and new tortures in the concentration camps of Europe."

He had said that "twice as many Negroes as whites are in combat," adding that this was a reflection of the Negro's position in America.

Dr. King's Response

BY LAWRENCE E. DAVIES | APRIL 13, 1967

LOS ANGELES, APRIL 12 — The Rev. Dr. Martin Luther King Jr. challenged today the National Association for the Advancement of Colored People to take a "forthright stand on the rightness or wrongness" of the Vietnam war.

Participating in news conferences at the Biltmore Hotel and at Occidental College here, Dr. King said he was "saddened" that the N.A.A.C.P. "would join in the perpetuation" of a "myth."

The "myth," he said, is that he advocates the fusion of the civil rights and peace drives. "I hold no such view," he said.

Dr. King explained his position as this: He personally will continue to take part in both movements but the Southern Christian Leadership Conference will remain concentrated on civil rights.

Money contributed for civil rights will not be used for peace advocacy, he said. He added that "no mechanical merger" would be involved.

"We do not believe in any merger or fusion of movements," Dr. King said, "but we equally believe that no one can pretend that the existence of the war is not profoundly affecting the destiny of civil rights progress."

Before today's statement in Los Angeles, Dr. King had spoken three times on the Vietnam war. At a rally in Chicago on March 25, he called on "all those who love peace" to "combine the fervor of the civil rights movement with the peace movement."

On March 30, in Louisville, Ky., the board of directors of the Southern Christian Leadership Conference adopted a resolution condemning United States conduct of the war. The board termed the war "morally and politically unjust" and said it had "drowned the Negro's cry for equal rights."

And in New York on April 4, Dr. King called on Negroes and "all white people of good will" to boycott the war by becoming conscientious objectors to military service.

Referring to Dr. [Ralph J.] Bunche's remarks today [that "Dr. King should positively and publicly give up one role or the other .... The two efforts have too little in common."] Dr. King asserted that he was "not going to quit either [role] positively or publicly."

"I shall remain as president of the Southern Christian Leadership Conference and do all I can in that role," he declared. "We will continue to work in Chicago and the South. But I deem it my responsibility to speak out positively and forthrightly on the war in Vietnam."

Told that some of his severest critics were saying he was placing all of the blame for the war on the United States, Dr. King replied: "We initiated the buildup of this war on land, on sea and in the air and we must make the initiative to end the war. I am not whitewashing Hanoi. I am a nonviolence believer .... "

Dr. King was asked whether he now thought that he had spoken too strongly last week when he compared United States actions in Vietnam with those of the Nazis during World War II.

In his New York speech, Dr. King said: "What do the peasants think as we ally ourselves with the landlords and as we refuse to put any action into our many words concerning land reform? What do they think as we test out our latest weapons on them, just as the Germans tested out new medicine and new tortures in the concentration camps of Europe?"

In response to the question today, he said:

"I did not make a general comparison. I merely said some things being done — the use of new weapons and medicines — were 'reminiscent' of World War II actions. We are testing new medicines and new weapons. We are using napalm. Everybody knows it.

"The United States at the moment is practicing more violence" than any other country, he declared, adding that he "made it very clear" in his remarks last week that he "did not compare the war in Vietnam to Hitler and what he did to the Jews."

Dr. King and the War

BY GENE ROBERTS | APRIL 14, 1967

ATLANTA, APRIL 13 — The outspoken stand of the Rev. Dr. Martin Luther King Jr. on the war in Vietnam has dampened his prospects for becoming the Negro leader who might be able to get the nation "moving again" on civil rights.

He now seems further removed than at any point in his career from leaders of the political establishment, the Urban League and the National Association for the Advancement of Colored People, and also from the mass of voters. He needs the support of all of these groups to win new gains for the Negro.

At the same time, Dr. King's attacks on the war appear to have won him only superficial support from young Negro militants who had found his approach on civil rights issues too conventional for their taste.

Ironically, Dr. King seems to have joined in the attack on the war, at least in part, because he thought it would help rather than hurt the civil rights efforts.

In recent months, as the civil rights movement became increasingly fragmented and directionless, Dr. King convinced himself that the nation was incapable of dealing simultaneously with two major issues.

WAR SEEN AS FIRST STEP

Thus, he reasoned, he would have to grapple with the war issue and help bring it to a satisfactory conclusion before he could make new headway on civil rights.

But in speaking out against the war, he has had to sacrifice his middle ground position among civil rights leaders. And it was precisely this position that had made Dr. King appear to so invaluable to those who had hoped they could build a new civil rights coalition around him.

When the civil rights movement flew apart last year over the "black power" issue, Dr. King stuck to the middle road by deploring black power but refusing to join the Urban League and the N.A.A.C.P. in denouncing such black power adherents as the Student Nonviolent Coordinating Committee and the Congress of Racial Equality.

Instead of denouncing the two organizations, Dr. King simply said he would not appear on the same platform with leaders of the two organizations as long as they were espousing what might be interpreted as an "antiwhite" position.

Without Dr. King by their sides, as he was in the civil rights march through Mississippi last summer, the black power organizations found it increasingly difficult to get funds and publicity.

By early this year, many civil rights supporters thought the "folly" of black power had been amply demonstrated and that the climate was now ripe for Dr. King to lead militants and moderates back into a new civil rights coalition.

But then Dr. King began his bitter denunciation of the war and almost immediately the hopes for a new coalition evaporated. For in attacking the war, Dr. King automatically aligned himself with the black power wing of the civil rights movement, which had long preached against the war, and cut himself adrift from the moderate wing of the movement.

On Saturday, for example, Dr. King will find himself doing what he once said he would not do. He will be speaking (at an anti-Vietnam rally in New York) from the same platform with such black power leaders as Stokely Carmichael of the Student Committee and Floyd B. McKissick of CORE.

This alone would be enough to disturb the more conservative leaders of the Urban League and the N.A.A.C.P. But they are even more concerned that the public will interpret Dr. King's statements on the war as being a fusion between civil rights and the peace movement and that this will accelerate what already seems to be growing popular disinterest in civil rights causes.

The N.A.A.C.P. voiced its fear in a public statement in which it called Dr. King's stand a "serious tactical mistake," And Dr. Ralph J.

Bunche, a member of the N.A.A.C.P.'s board of directors, expanded on the statement Wednesday.

"In my view, Dr. King should positively and publicly give up one role or the other," Dr. Bunche said. "The two efforts have too little in common."

Dr. King immediately replied that it was possible for him to speak out as an individual without fusing civil rights and Vietnam protests.

But until a few weeks ago, interestingly enough, he held exactly the same position as the N.A.A.CP. and Dr. Bunche.

In late 1965, after airing his "moral misgivings" about the war in a speech in Virginia, he told associates that the resentment aroused by the speech had convinced him that he could not continue to speak out against the war without harming the civil rights cause.

As important as the war was, Dr. King went on at the time, it was more important for him to be able to fashion a program around which all the various supporters of civil rights could coalesce.

FEARED WRONG GOALS

He felt that unless this was done the entire civil rights movement was in danger of exhausting its energies in rivalries and in seeking goals that would be of only secondary importance to Negroes.

There was a period of several months last year in which Dr. King thought he had found just the sort of goal — a guaranteed income for Negroes — that would once again get the civil rights movement working together in harmony.

However, after several weeks of meditation and book writing in Jamaica earlier this year, he decided upon an all-out attack on the war.

While he is attacking, it is clear, an already weak civil rights movement is growing weaker, and an already disinterested public is growing increasingly disinterested.

Meanwhile, civil rights advocates are waiting in the wings, hoping against hope for the sort of program that has eluded them since the passage of the Voting Rights Act of 1964. But it does not appear to be coming from Dr. King.

100,000 Rally at U. N. Against Vietnam War

BY DOUGLAS ROBINSON | APRIL 16, 1967

THOUSANDS OF antiwar demonstrators marched through the streets of Manhattan yesterday and then massed in front of the United Nations building to hear United States policy in Vietnam denounced.

The Police Department's office of Community Relations said that police officers at the scene estimated the number of demonstrators outside the United Nations at "between 100,000 and 125,000."

It was difficult to make any precise count because people were continually leaving and entering the rally area. It was also almost impossible to distinguish the demonstrators from passersby and spectators.

On Friday the police had announced that they were prepared for a crowd of 100,000 to 400,000.

LEADERS OF PARADE

It was the largest peace demonstration staged in New York since the Vietnam war began. It took four hours for all the marchers to leave Central Park for the United Nations Plaza.

The parade was led by the Rev. Dr. Martin Luther King Jr., Dr. Benjamin Spock, the pediatrician, and Harry Belafonte, the singer, as well as several other civil rights and religious figures, all of whom linked arms as they moved out of the park at the head of the line.

The marchers — who had poured into New York in chartered buses, trains and cars from cities as far away as Pittsburgh, Cleveland and Chicago — included housewives from Westchester, students and poets from the Lower East Side, priests and nuns, doctors, businessmen and teachers.

JACK MANNING/THE NEW YORK TIMES

The Rev. Dr. Martin Luther King Jr. addresses the antiwar rally outside the United Nations.

CHANTS FROM YOUTHS

As they began trooping out of Central Park toward Fifth Avenue, some of the younger demonstrators changed: "Hell no, we won't go," and "Hey, Hey, L. B. J., How Many Kids Did You Kill Today."

Most of the demonstrators, however, marched silently as they passed equally silent crowds of onlookers. Other blocks were almost deserted.

Some of the marchers were hit with eggs and red paint. At 47th Street and Park Avenue, several demonstrators were struck by steel rods from a building under construction. Some plastic cups filled with sand barely missed another group. There were no serious injuries.

At least five persons were arrested for disorderly conduct. Three youths were taken into custody when they tried to rush a float that depicted the Statue of Liberty.

The demonstration here and a similar one in San Francisco were sponsored by the Spring Mobilization Committee to End the War in Vietnam, a loose confederation of leftwing, pacifist and moderate anti-war groups.

A few minutes before 11 A.M., an hour before the parade started, about 70 young men gathered on an outcropping of rock in the south-east corner of the Sheep Meadow in Central Park to burn their draft cards. They were quickly joined by others, some of whom appeared to have decided to join in on the spot.

HARD TO CHECK

The demonstrators said that nearly 200 cards were burned, although in the chanting, milling throng it was impossible to get an accurate count or to tell whether all the papers burned were draft cards.

Surrounded by a human chain that kept out hundreds of onlookers, the demonstrators first clustered in small groups around cigarette lighters, then sat down and passed cards up to a youth holding a flaming coffee can. Cheers and chants of "Resist, Resist" went up as small white cards — many of which were passed hand to hand from outside the circle caught fire.

Many of the demonstrators carried or wore daffodils and chanted "Flower Power."

It was the first large draft card burning in the protests against the war in Vietnam, although groups of up to a dozen had publicly burned their cards.

Among the group yesterday was a youth in the uniform, jump boots and green beret of the Army Special Forces, whose name tag said "Rader." He identified himself as Gary Rader of Evanston, Ill., and said he had served a year and a half of active duty as a reservist.

Like the rest of the demonstrators, the card burners were a mixed group. Most were of college age, and included bearded, button-wearing hippies, earnest students in tweed coats and ties, and youths who fitted in neither category.

There were a number of girls who burned half of their husband's or boyfriend's draft cards while the men burned the other half. Among the burners were a sprinkling of older men, including several veterans and the Rev. Thomas Hayes of the Episcopal Peace Fellowship.

Last week the United States Court of Appeals for the First Circuit held unconstitutional a law passed in 1965 banning draft-card burning under pain of a maximum 5-year sentence and a $10,000 fine: Two convictions under the law, however, have been upheld by United States Courts of Appeals in the Second and Eighth Circuits.

VIETCONG FLAGS RAISED

In his speech at the United Nations rally, Dr. King repeatedly called on the United States to "honor its word" and "stop the bombing of North Vietnam."

"I would like to urge students from colleges all over the nation to use this summer and coming summers educating and organizing communities across the nation against war," Dr. King told the crowd.

Before making his speech, the minister and a five-man delegation presented a formal note to Dr. Ralph Bunche, Undersecretary for Special Political Affairs at the United Nations.

The note said: "We rally at the United Nations in order to affirm support of the principals of peace, universality, equal rights and self-determination of peoples embodied in the Charter and acclaimed by mankind, but violated by the United States."

The demonstrators began to assemble in Central Park's Sheep Meadow early in the morning.

On one grassy knoll, a group calling itself the United States Committee to Aid the National Liberation Front of South Vietnam built a 40-foot high tower of black cardboard tubing. They then attached a number of Liberation Front (Vietcong) flags of blue and red with a gold star in the center.

At 12:20 P.M., the parade stepped off from Central Park South and the Avenue of the Americas, with Dr. King and the other leaders in the vanguard. They were surrounded by a group of parade marshals who linked hands to shield them from possible violence. From the hundreds of people lining the route of march came expressions of anger or support.

"I think it's terrible," said Carl Hoffman, an engineer from Hartford, who stood at the corner where the march began.

Nearby, 20-year-old Estelle Klein, an office manager from Queens, gazed at the students, nuns, businessmen, veterans and doctors marching by and said: "I'd be out there too, but I don't know, I just don't think it'll do any good."

As the demonstrators moved east on 59th Street, they encountered bands of youths carrying American flags and hoisting placards with such slogans as "Bomb Hanoi" and "Dr. Spock Smokes Bananas."

The bands of youths ran along the sidewalks paralleling the line of march, calling insults at the demonstrators.

Along one stretch of high-rise apartment houses on Lexington Avenue, eggs were dumped from a number of windows and many marchers had their clothes stained with red paint tossed by persons behind police barricades.

GUESTS PEER OUT

From the windows of the Barbizon-Plaza Hotel, the Plaza and the St. Moritz, guests — a few still in pajamas — peered from their rooms at the throng moving out of the park. Most of these watchers neither applauded nor heckled.

Although the demonstrators were supposed to follow a line of march set up by the police, several thousand members of the Harlem contingent broke away and marched down Seventh Avenue through Times Square.

Several fistfights broke out in Times Square between angry motorists caught in a huge traffic jam and the paraders.

At 42d Street and Second Avenue, a fight broke out between several spectators and 19-year-old Edward Katz of Manhattan. Mr. Katz said later that he was trying to get to his car with his wife and baby when "a group of antipeace people started knocking over the baby carriage."

By 4 P.M., the last of the marchers had moved out of Central Park, leaving it looking like a disaster area. The paths and roadways were covered with litter.

There were several floats in the parade, including one on which Pete Seeger, the folk singer, rode with a number of children. They sang folk songs like "This Land Is Your Land" as they rolled along the line of march.

Most of the marchers carried signs that had been authorized and printed by the Spring Mobilization Committee. Among the slogans were "Stop the Bombing," "No Vietnamese Ever Called Me Nigger" and "Children Are Not Born to Burn."

There were many unauthorized banners and placards, however. One, a bed sheet carried by three young men, bore in large black letters the words, "Ho Chi Minh is a Virgin."

A minor scuffle between the police and the peace marchers broke out at 3 P.M. on the south side of 42d Street just west of First Avenue when some marchers tried to turn north.

Patrolmen on foot moved into the crowd, trying to push them into line. Other policemen on horseback charged into the throng and helped turn the marchers back. Nearby, counter-demonstrators screamed: "Kill them, kill them."

The speeches at the United Nations did not start until after 2 P.M. While the demonstrators waited, filling the plaza from 47th to 42d Streets, they were entertained by folk singers.

An overflow crowd filled the side streets west of First Avenue.

More than 2,000 policemen were on hand at the United Nations to keep order, and to separate demonstrators from counter-demonstrators.

'BE-IN' AT THE PARK

A "be-in" of several thousand young men and women preceded the start of the parade. They gathered on a rock out-cropping in the southeast corner of the Sheep Meadow, dancing and singing to the music of guitars, flutes and drums.

Many of the young people had painted their faces and legs with poster paint. The sweet smell of cooking bananas hung over the group.

Unidentified demonstrators set fire to an American flag held up on a flagstaff in the park before the march began, the police said. No arrests were made in connection with the incident.

After leaving Dr. Bunche's office at the United Nations, Dr. King told newsmen that the demonstration was "just a beginning of a massive outpouring of concern and protest activity against this illegal and unjust war."

The speeches ended soon after 5 P.M. when a downpour drenched the plaza, converting it into a field of soggy clothing, peeling placards and deep puddles. The rally area was almost completely deserted by 6:30, except for crews from the Sanitation Department who were cleaning up a mountain of debris.

Speakers at the rally, in addition to Dr. King, included Floyd McKissick, national secretary of the Congress of Racial Equality, and Stokely Carmichael, leader of the Student Non-Violent Coordinating Committee.

Mr. Carmichael, who spoke against background shouts of "black power," described the United States presence in Vietnam as "brutal and racist," and declared that he was against "drafting young men, particularly young black Americans."

Mr. McKissick called for the immediate withdrawal of American troops from Vietnam and predicted that the turnout of marchers would bring "some positive, action" from Washington.

The Rev. James Bevel, who was national director of Spring Mobilization, said he would give President Johnson "one month to stop murdering those folks in Vietnam."

"That's all we'll give him, one month to pull those guns out," Mr. Bevel said with his fists upraised. "If he doesn't, we'll close down New York City." He did not elaborate.

Before leaving Central Park, Mr. Belafonte told newsmen that he was participating in the demonstration because "the war in Vietnam — like all wars — is immoral."

CHAPTER 4

The Need for Civil Disobedience

Dr. King's message of peace and justice resonated throughout the nation. He once again garnered enormous support, this time at antiwar rallies and peace protests. He declined the request to run for president, citing the need to remain nonpartisan to more effectively work toward resolving poverty and inequality. He made plans for a massive civil rights demonstration in Washington, D.C. And he led a protest march in Memphis that, against his wishes, turned violent. Dr. King redoubled his commitment to nonviolent resistance and planned a second march in Memphis.

King Warns Cities of Summer Riots

BY DOUGLAS ROBINSON | APRIL 17, 1967

THE REV. DR. MARTIN LUTHER KING JR. warned yesterday that at least 10 cities across the country, including New York, could "explode in racial violence this summer."

Describing the cities as "powder kegs," he said "the nation has not done anything to improve conditions in these areas."

"I'll still preach nonviolence with all my might, but I'm afraid it will fall on deaf ears," he said.

Dr. King, speaking at an impromptu news conference, included among the cities Cleveland, Chicago, Los Angeles, Oakland, Calif., Washington, Newark and New York. He said there were other cities, which he did not name, in the South.

The civil rights figure, who led a massive antiwar demonstration here on Saturday, said any outbreaks in New York could occur in either Harlem or the Bedford-Stuyvesant section of Brooklyn.

Last summer, there were racial disturbances in Chicago, Cleveland, the San Francisco Bay area, and Bedford-Stuyvesant.

Dr. King said he was particularly fearful of possible riots in Southern cities. "We haven't had any riots in the South yet, and conditions are intolerable down there," he said.

"I'm sorry to have to say this," he went on, "but the intolerable conditions which brought about racial violence last summer still exist."

ASSAILS CROWD ESTIMATE

Dr. King challenged a police estimate that between 100,000 and 125,000 people took part in the rally outside the United Nations building here Saturday.

"I have no quarrel with the police estimate," he said with a slight smile, "just an absolute denial of the accuracy of it."

Dr. King, who said he had been taking part in demonstrations for years and had had wide experience in estimating the size of crowds, "perhaps more experience than the New York police," declared: "There were fully 300,000 and perhaps 400,000 people in the demonstration."

"I spoke to as many of 125,000 persons in the United Nations plaza," he said, "and then I went back to Central Park. There were that many people still marching.

"Too often we find that when there is an issue that the police or the press are against, they play down the number of people involved. When it is an issue they favor, they add to the total number."

Deputy Police Commissioner Jacques Nevard, who is in charge of police press relations, said yesterday that "we certainly won't get into any discussion of the figures."

"We issue no official figures in the first place," Mr. Nevard commented. "Reporters simply know that police officers will very often make unofficial estimates."

Speaking of the demonstration, Mayor Lindsay, in his weekly radio broadcast over WNYC last night, praised the police for the "superb way they handled this rather difficult problem."

"There were a few minor instances of disruption, but they were not serious," he said. "Only in New York City could you handle a group of over 100,000 with that ease."

Dr. King decried a disclosure by George Christian, White House press secretary, that the Federal Bureau of Investigation was keeping an eye on "antiwar activity."

He termed any investigation of the peace movement "totally unnecessary," and added that "the people protesting the war by and large are patriotic Americans."

TALKS ABOUT COMMUNISM

"There are 15 million Americans who actively oppose the war and millions of others who are not in sympathy with it," he said. "I challenge anybody to say that all these people are Communists."

Later in the day, in an appearance on the National Broadcasting Company program "Meet the Press," Secretary of State Dean Rusk said the "Communist apparatus" was busy in support of antiwar demonstrations. He added: "But I do not mean to say by that all those who have objections to the war in Vietnam are Communists."

Earlier, speaking on the Columbia Broadcasting System program "Face the Nation," Dr. King declared that he was philosophically opposed to communism.

He said: "I think it is based on a metaphysical materialism, at points an ethical relativism, a crippling totalitarianism in many instances and a denial of human freedom that I would not prefer."

He also disassociated the sponsors of the antiwar demonstration from the burning of draft cards and an American flag. He said the Spring Mobilization Committee to End the War in Vietnam, which organized the rally, could not "condone" such actions.

Meantime, most of the thousands who came here from out of town for the demonstration had left the city. In many cases, the special trains and chartered buses that brought them here from such points as Pittsburgh, Cleveland and Chicago, left Saturday night.

There were still some visitors, however. At noon yesterday, in the Sheep Meadow in Central Park, where thousands had milled Saturday before the peace parade started, a baseball game was in progress.

Anshel Bruston of Cincinnati, who was catching for one team, said, "We're all playing before we go home."

"It's Cincy versus Detroit," he explained, adding that all 15 persons playing had been in the march. At the time, Cincinnati was leading 7 to 1 in the bottom of the fifth, with Detroit at bat.

Dr. King Is Backed for Peace Ticket

BY PAUL HOFMANN | APRIL 22, 1967

LEADING OPPONENTS of the war in Vietnam said yesterday that they hoped that the Rev. Dr. Martin Luther King Jr. would agree to run as an independent Presidential candidate on a peace platform next year.

At the very least, they said they did not expect the civil rights leader and Nobel Peace prize winner to block a draft movement.

Dr. Benjamin Spock, the pediatrician, was mentioned as a possible running mate for Dr. King.

"We are negotiating with Dr. King" about a possible Presidential campaign, William F. Pepper, executive director of the National Conference for New Politics, said yesterday. The leftist group was established last year to bring opponents of the war in Vietnam into politics.

RAMPARTS TO APPEAL TO HIM

Robert Scheer, managing editor of Ramparts magazine, also said that he had been in contact with Dr. King with a view to winning his consent to be a peace candidate for the Presidency "in next year's general election, not just in the primaries." Mr. Scheer said that his magazine, in its May issue, to be published next week, would appeal to Dr. King to run for President.

Dr. King was quoted by an aide in Atlanta last night as expressing "extreme reluctance to get involved directly in politics." On the other hand, he was quoted as having said that he "understands very much the objectives of these groups" promoting his candidacy.

Dr. King completed a routine medical checkup in Atlanta last night.

His aide, the Rev. Andrew Young, remarked that "much will depend on the state of the union — whether the war in Vietnam is over, et cetera — in the early part of 1968 — let's say January or February."

Mr. Young is the executive director of the Southern Christian Leadership Conference, of which Dr. King is chairman.

TO OPEN 'VIETNAM SUMMER'

Dr. King is scheduled to meet with Dr. Spock and would-be promoters of his candidacy in Cambridge, Mass., tomorrow. The occasion is the start of a nationwide "Vietnam Summer" organizing effort. The project is aimed at channeling opposition to the war in Vietnam into political action. The effort is patterned on the Freedom Summer in 1964 when volunteers went to Mississippi for civil rights activities.

Both Mr. Pepper and Mr. Scheer said in separate interviews yesterday that they would discuss Dr. King's possible candidacy with him in Cambridge.

The idea was mentioned publicly by Mr. Pepper in a speech last Saturday in New York during the "spring mobilization" against the war in Vietnam. It was learned that Dr. King had been told that Mr. Pepper was going to propose him as a Presidential candidate, and had no objection, provided that Mr. Pepper spoke after he did. Dr. King gave the main address at the rally in front of United Nations headquarters.

'MAYBE NEXT FIRST LADY'

Mrs. Coretta King, Dr. King's wife, was introduced as "maybe the next First Lady" when she spoke simultaneously at an antiwar rally in Kezar Stadium in San Francisco. Mrs. King was presented to the audience by John Burton, a San Francisco city councilman.

Dr. King's candidacy may be promoted both inside and outside the Democratic party, Mr. Pepper and Mr. Scheer suggested.

"To get him on the ballot in California as an independent, we need 67,000 signatures," Mr. Scheer said. "There's no problem getting these signatures."

Dr. King Declines Peace Candidacy

BY WALTER RUGABER | APRIL 26, 1967

ATLANTA, APRIL 25 — The Rev. Dr. Martin Luther King Jr. reiterated his support of the peace movement today but announced that he would not be its candidate for President in 1968.

"I understand the stirrings across the country for a candidate who will take a firm, principled stand on the question of the war in Vietnam and the problem of the poor in urban ghettos," he said, "but I must also add that I have no interest in being that candidate."

He made the announcement at a news conference in the Ebenezer Baptist Church, where he is co-pastor. The Negro leader, who is president of the Southern Christian Leadership Conference and a winner of the Nobel Peace Prize, had been urged to run for President by some leaders of the opposition to the war.

"I have come to think of my role as one which operates outside the realm of partisan politics," he said, "raising the issues and through action creating the situation which forces whatever party is in power to act creatively and constructively in response to the dramatic presentations of these issues on the public scene."

"I plan to continue that role in the hope that the war in Vietnam will be brought to a close long before the 1968 election, and that this present Congress will find both the courage and the votes to once again move our nation toward a truly great society for every citizen."

He attacked Gen. William C. Westmoreland, the United States military commander in Vietnam, who said yesterday that antiwar protests encouraged the enemy.

"I think this sinister, evil attempt to confuse the minds of the American people must be stopped," Dr. King said. "What prolongs the war is not opposition to the war but our continued escalation of the war."

At the meeting, Chester Jennings, chairman of the Board of Aldermen, said the open-housing supporters had agreed on a "30 to 60 day moratorium" on demonstrations, assuring there would be no disruption of the Kentucky Derby [in Louisville, Ky.] next week.

But Dr. King said declaration was "entirely incorrect."

Dr. King also said plans were in effect for a "drive-in" on Thursday aimed at snarling traffic in the downtown area.

Civil Rights; King Sees a Dual Mission

BY GENE ROBERTS | MAY 7, 1967

ATLANTA — For a while some Negroes and sympathetic whites held out hope that the Rev. Dr. Martin Luther King Jr. might say what he had to say about the war in Vietnam, and then turn his undivided attention back to civil rights.

But last week, Dr. King made it clear that this is not going to happen as long as the war is in progress. He told his congregation at Ebenezer Baptist Church in Atlanta that civil rights supporters who criticize him for his stand against the war never really understood him in the first place. He said that as "a minister of God" and as a winner of the Nobel Peace Prize he has a "mission to work harder for peace," and he plans to do just that.

Then he went on to praise boxer Cassius Clay and others who refuse to submit to the draft, and to charge that President Johnson had brought Gen. William C. Westmoreland home from Vietnam to silence dissent."

All of this means that Southern Negroes, who have come to look toward Dr. King for aid in their civil rights battles, can expect little of it this year — barring some major catastrophe such as the Birmingham church bombing four years ago. With his escalation of the peace offensive and his commitment to a civil rights program in Chicago, he has neither the time nor the organizational resources.

WRITING OFF SOUTH

Hosea Williams, one of Dr. King's top aides, acknowledged this recently when asked if Dr. King's Southern Christian Leadership Conference "has written off the South."

"I wouldn't put it quite that way, because we're still interested in the South," Mr. Williams said. "But I guess that is what it amounts to."

Already the civil rights movement — in the sense that it is built around professional civil rights workers and outside volunteers — has collapsed in all but a handful of Southern counties. And Dr. King's commitment to the antiwar effort dims the prospects of the movement's reviving in the region anytime soon.

But as Dr. King appears to see it, the civil rights struggle cannot really be won anyway until the war is settled. He has said in interviews that much of the nation has turned its back on such Negro problems as poverty in order to wage the war, and that this is one reason he has become increasingly active in the peace movement.

NONVIOLENCE THE ANSWER

Among his other reasons: he believes that the war is unjust and that nonviolence, not violence, is the answer to international problems. However, in his sermon to his Atlanta congregation, he said he might have temporarily dropped his pacifism in World War II, had he been of military age, "because Hitler was such an evil force."

So opposed has Dr. King become to the war in Vietnam, in fact, that he has drawn closer to such "black power" organizations as the Student Nonviolent Coordinating Committee and the Congress of Racial Equality which have been actively opposing the war for more than a year. This alliance is a step he once said he would not take as long as the two organizations advocated a doctrine that could be interpreted as racial separation, but now he seems to feel that the peace effort outweighs other considerations.

For their part, the student committee and CORE reject Dr. King's hard-and-fast adherence to nonviolence in the civil rights struggle, but welcome it when applied to the anti-war movement. Last week for example, Stokely Carmichael, the student committee chairman, attended Dr. King's sermon in Atlanta and interrupted him twice with applause.

What impact will Dr. King's opposition to the war and association with black-power leaders have upon his own effectiveness as a civil rights leader?

It doesn't seem likely that it will affect his standing with the mass of Negroes, including many of those who vigorously support the war effort. "I'm a veteran and I support the country's position in Vietnam." Clyde Banks, a Negro grocer in Chatham, Va., said last week in what seems to be a typical reaction. "But I still think Martin Luther King is the greatest living American."

DIFFERENT IMPACT

But leaders of the National Association for the Advancement of Colored People think the impact is quite different on Congress, and upon many whites who support civil rights programs, but also favor the country's position in Vietnam. And resentment from these groups could prevent Dr. King from ever molding another effective civil rights coalition.

Ironically, Dr. King himself once thought it a mistake to mix Vietnam and civil rights, and kept quiet about the war throughout last year.

The Voice of Negro Leadership

BY THE NEW YORK TIMES | JULY 27, 1967

FOUR VETERAN civil rights leaders have laid their reputations and their careers on the line in joining President Johnson's plea for public order and in forthrightly condemning those who are attempting to lead the Negro community down the primrose path of arson, looting and murder.

The statement issued yesterday by the Rev. Martin Luther King Jr., A. Philip Randolph, Roy Wilkins and Whitney M. Young Jr. is courageous and wise, a timely act of responsible citizenship that deserves the respect and active support of Negroes and whites alike.

In rejecting unequivocally violence as a means to racial justice — "there is no injustice which justifies the present destruction…" — these four moderate Negro leaders have made a clean break with the extremists and the latter's mindless followers.

In making this break, the moderates have had to abandon recent attempts to achieve a broad unity in the civil rights movement that would have enabled them to channel the energies of the brash young "black power" rabble-rousers into constructive channels. The decision must have been an agonizing one, but it was inescapable for men of conscience in the light of the events in Detroit and other cities and of the blatantly inflammatory speech delivered by Student Nonviolent Coordinating Committee leader H. Rapp Brown in Cambridge, Md.

But in this time of rising frustration and hysteria in the ghetto, the success of this bold bid to return the movement for racial equality to legitimate paths may depend most of all on the response of the white community. Unless the whites who continue to dominate the economic and political life of this biracial nation begin to respond more positively to the legitimate demands long peacefully pressed by such responsible Negro leaders as those who issued yesterday's statement, the voice of the Negro community will increasingly be the incendiary voice of the H. Rapp Browns. That way lies disaster for Negro and white alike.

Dr. King Stresses Pride in His Race

BY GENE ROBERTS | AUG. 19, 1967

ATLANTA, AUG. 18 — The Southern Christian Leadership Conference, fighting to hold its own against the growing black power movement, has begun placing heavy emphasis on black consciousness and racial pride.

This development became clear here this week at the annual convention of the civil rights organization headed by the Rev. Dr. Martin Luther King Jr.

Large placards that said "Black is beautiful and it's so beautiful to be black" decked the walls of the convention meeting rooms at the Ebenezer Baptist Church. And speaker after speaker — including Dr. King — called for black ownership and control of Negro ghettos and laced their speeches with such phrases as a "sense of negritude" and "Afro-American unity."

Dr. King, while continuing to campaign for integration, also urged the reconstruction of the English language to upgrade the word "black." He offered no explanation as to how this could be done.

He said he recently checked a thesaurus and found more than 60 of 120 synonyms for black to be offensive, while all 134 synonyms for white were favorable.

A DIFFERENCE IN LYING

"They even tell us," he added, "that a white lie is better than a black lie."

One of Dr. King's chief aides, the Rev. Bernard Lee, showed up for the convention wearing his hair in what has come to be called the "natural African style."

Another aide, the Rev. James Bevel, said that his quarrel with such black power leaders as Stokely Carmichael was not so much over the racial overtones in their speeches as over their calls for violence.

The entire convention joined in the black consciousness drive, unanimously passing a resolution that calls for a series of "identity workshops" and “Afro-American unity conferences.” The conferences would, as one delegate explained, include all segment of the Negro community — the “revolutionary, the militant and the churchman.”

Dr. King said that such conferences were necessary to “establish a dialogue” and insure that nonviolence wins out in the end over violence as a method of Negro protest.

Dr. King’s organization made a greater effort this year than in the past to attract white speakers and supporters to its annual convention. Whites made up about a fifth of the 1,400 people who attended the convention’s opening banquet.

The white speakers included Ralph McGill, publisher of The Atlanta Constitution; the Right Rev. James A. Pike of the Episcopal Church, and Ivan Allen, Mayor of Atlanta. Mr. Allen’s speech marked the first time in the conference’s 10-year history that its convention delegates were welcomed to a city by a Mayor.

However, Willie Ricks, one of the Student Nonviolent Coordinating Committee’s angriest advocates of violence and black power, also attended the convention.

Convention officials invited Cassius Clay, the boxer, to speak. But Clay, who is also known by his Black Muslim name, Muhammad Ali, did not show up.

Some of Dr. King’s staff members say that he must by necessity “play both sides of the street,” (woo black power supporters as well as white moderates and liberals) if he is to build a national consensus for his favorite goal — a guaranteed annual income for the impoverished.

He must also, they add, be careful to cultivate both middle class and lower income Negroes if he is to continue to have a broad following among members of his race.

This, his aides concede, leads at times to complications and what appears to be contradictions in the way Dr. King runs his organization.

On the one hand, his organization provided bus transportation for impoverished Mississippi and Alabama Negroes who wanted to come to the convention.

On the other hand, Dr. King held the convention's major banquet at Atlanta's newest hotel, the Regency-Hyatt House, to stimulate $10 a plate ticket sales among middle class Negroes.

Dr. King Planning To Disrupt Capital In Drive for Jobs

BY WALTER RUGABER | DEC. 5, 1967

ATLANTA, DEC. 4 — The Rev. Dr. Martin Luther King Jr. announced plans today to lead an extended campaign of massive civil disobedience in Washington next year to force Congress and the Administration to provide "jobs or income for all."

The internationally known Negro civil rights leader said a force of 3,000 demonstrators, trained in nonviolent techniques, would seek "massive dislocation" of the capital "until America responds" to the needs of its poor.

Dr. King said the protesters, recruited in 10 major cities and five rural areas, would begin a "strong, dramatic, and attention-getting campaign" in early April. He indicated that the Capitol and the White House would be among the targets.

CAMPAIGN CALLED 'RISKY'

In a news conference here, the winner of the Nobel Prize for Peace acknowledged that the ugly mood of many Negroes in the nation's slums made the campaign "risky," but he asserted that "not to act represents moral irresponsibility."

Dr. King advanced the view that "angry and bitter" people would respond to nonviolence "if it's militant enough, if it's really doing something." He promised to spend three months in training the initial force of 3,000.

"These tactics have done it [won civil rights advances] before," Dr. King said, "and this is all we have to go on." Continued inaction by the Federal Government, he warned, will bring down "the curtain of doom" upon the nation.

For some time, Dr. King has been talking generally about the dislocation of Northern cities "without destroying life or property." Such efforts, he has said, can channel rage from destructive rioting to more "creative" ends.

The Negro leader committed himself most firmly to the idea of dislocation during a speech in August to the annual convention of the Southern Christian Leadership Conference. He is president of the Atlanta-based group.

Then, last week. Dr. King and the leading members of his staff chose Washington as the target and mapped other aspects of the projected drive during a meeting at Frogmore, S. C. In a statement issued today, Dr. King said:

"America is at a crossroads of history, and it is critically important for us, as a nation and a society, to choose a new path and move upon it with resolution and courage.

"It is impossible to underestimate the crisis we face in America. The stability of a civilization, the potential of free government, and the simple honor of men are at stake."

Dr. King said that "a clear majority in America are asking for the very things which we will demand in Washington," but he added that the Government "does not move to correct the problem involving race until it is confronted directly and dramatically."

The Negro leader's mood seemed deeply pessimistic. He said the confrontation in Washington was a "last desperate demand" by Negroes, an attempt to avoid "the worst chaos, hatred and violence any nation has ever encountered."

A number of details concerning the new drive apparently remained unsettled. Dr. King said the areas from which the demonstrators would come had not been chosen, although Mississippi and New York have been mentioned. Some of the protesters may march to Washington, Dr. King said.

THE FORMS OF PROTEST

An aide to the civil rights leader said that financial needs would present no problem. The protesters would camp out, he indicated, and "soup kitchens" might be organized for them at various churches in Washington.

While Dr. King avoided detailing the forms of protest that might be used, other sources suggested transportation tie-ups, school boycotts and appearances at major Government installations in the capital.

One aide, citing the high incidence of infant mortality among Negroes, said another tactic might be to tie up Washington hospitals with waves of sick youngsters. Such action, he said, would be useful as well as dramatic.

Dr. King said he hoped the new campaign would involve representatives of the non-Negro poor and "all Americans of good will." An aide added, however, that the drive would need more or less permanent demonstrators, "not college kids down for a weekend."

Negro militants, including the Student Nonviolent Coordinating Committee, will be asked to participate, Dr. King said, but all participants in the protests must pledge nonviolence for the duration.

Dr. King said the peace movement would also be invited to participate on the grounds that many believe domestic poverty cannot be successfully fought until the Government withdraws from the war in Vietnam.

Dr. King to Train 3,000 as Leaders for Capital March

BY THE NEW YORK TIMES | JAN. 17, 1968

ATLANTA, JAN. 16 — The Rev. Dr. Martin Luther King Jr. said here today that the "massive mobilization for Washington" he plans to lead this April would be kept militant but nonviolent by a trained corps of 3,000 from six Southern states and nine Northern cities.

The goal of the mobilization, which he described as "going for broke," would be "a program that would provide either jobs or income for all Americans," Dr. King told a news conference at the Ebenezer Baptist Church. But specific demands and tactics are still being worked out, he said, and "the element of surprise" will be maintained.

The "core group," he said, is to be recruited and "trained in the discipline of nonviolence and what the mobilization is all about" by Southern Christian Leadership Conference field workers being instructed, here this week.

After the 3,000 have "set the nonviolent tone" of the demonstrations in Washington, Dr. King said, "we will escalate the campaign, bringing in thousands and thousands of people."

He said he expected these additional people to remain nonviolent as well. He has met with black nationalist leaders, he said, and told them "if you don't agree with nonviolence, at least let us go through with our plans." He pointed out that extreme militants had participated in Chicago demonstrations without violence.

The core group is to consist of some 200 members each from Mississippi, Alabama, Georgia, South Carolina, North Carolina, Virginia, Washington, Philadelphia, Newark, New York, Boston, Chicago, Cleveland, Baltimore and Detroit he announced.

Civil Rights; Strong Challenge by King

BY WALTER RUGABER | FEB. 11, 1968

NOT SINCE HUNDREDS of his followers marched from Selma to Montgomery almost three years ago has the Rev. Dr. Martin Luther King Jr. produced a crusade of national dimensions against racial discrimination.

But last week, while he was in Washington for a two-day antiwar mobilization of 2,500 Clergy and Laymen Concerned About Vietnam — which included a silent prayer vigil at Arlington National Cemetery — Dr. King was making plans for a massive civil rights demonstration in the nation's capital this April. And he indicated that the protest might move later to Chicago and Miami Beach for the national political conventions during the summer.

NEW GOAL

The goal of this new "March on Washington," Dr. King said, was to pressure Congress into enacting legislation that would guarantee employment or, for anyone unable to work, a decent income. "This just means adding about $10 billion to the [budget] deficit," the Negro leader estimated matter-of-factly last week. While no one expects even to approach that figure, many sympathizers warn that some progress is essential.

Dr. King believes the forthcoming effort to obtain economic relief for Negroes is the nation's last chance for nonviolent change. Dr. King's plan to mount a militant civil disobedience campaign in Washington this April is designed as a "constructive channel" for the anger and frustration that has erupted in many big cities since 1965.

The only alternative, he feels, is continued rebellion. And rioting not only destroys the lives and property of Negroes but also carries a rejection of the nonviolent philosophy Dr. King has successfully espoused for more than a decade.

Proposals for long-range economic efforts cannot take hold in time to prevent new outbreaks this summer, Dr. King's aides have argued, and each riot may strengthen the hand of extremist leaders such as Stokely Carmichael. Thus, the Washington campaign is aimed at obtaining an immediate Federal largesse for the poor, and offering Negroes a chance at more rational protest, and at sustaining Dr. King's leadership of the civil rights movement.

Will it work? The technique won widespread sympathy when employed against bitter-end segregationists In the South, but will it prove as successful when applied directly to the nation's capital In 1968? Most observers expect it to be a difficult business at best. The country seems hardly sympathetic to such a campaign. A number of political leaders in Washington and elsewhere have appeared distinctly cool.

"We'll do all we can to work with all groups, see that their views are heard, considered and acted upon," President Johnson declared earlier this month. But he suggested that the movement's efforts could be more productively directed.

ADMITTED RISK

Washington is a center of considerable black nationalist activity and many Negroes there are said to be in an ugly mood. Dr. King has acknowledged the risk that his nonviolent effort could itself generate rioting. But the failure to act, he reasoned, would practically guarantee disorder and discredit the standing of nonviolence. His staff at the Southern Christian Leadership Conference, which discussed the problems for months, ultimately agreed.

Dr. King envisions the Washington campaign as a bi-racial coalition of diverse groups and personalities. He began drumming up support last week by calling on Mr. Carmichael and other militants in Washington.

The demonstrations would be organized around a force of some 3,000 persons selected over the next two months from 10 cities and five rural areas around the country. All would be carefully trained in nonviolence, Dr. King has promised.

To guard further against setting off riots, Dr. King plans to require that others engaged in the campaign take a pledge of nonviolence for as long as they participate. This tactic has had an uncertain effect in some past instances.

"Dr. King is *still* the Negro leader, regardless of what the militants say," one person outside the leadership conference observed last week. "Most Negroes will move in his direction — if some concessions are made to him."

Dr. King to Start March on the Capital April 22

BY BEN A. FRANKLIN | MARCH 5, 1968

ATLANTA, MARCH 4 — The Rev. Dr. Martin Luther King Jr. today set Monday, April 22, as the starting date of his "nonviolent poor people's march on Washington." For the first time he decisively linked its antidiscrimination and antipoverty objectives to a campaign to end the war in Vietnam.

Dr. King, the president of the Southern Christian Leadership Conference, also introduced new and complex problems of transportation and protection of the demonstrators scheduled to converge on the capital from the South. He did this in disclosing plans for thousands to march — or to move in buses and by foot — over the highways in Mississippi, Alabama, Georgia, the Carolinas, Virginia and into the District of Columbia.

MARCH THROUGH ALABAMA

The line of march, he said, "symbolically would almost have to go from Selma to Montgomery," Ala., over U.S. Highway 80, the route of Dr. King's noted demonstration in 1965. That march cost the lives of two white participants, Mrs. Viola Liuzzo and the Rev. James Reeb.

In describing the logistics and the goals of the planned spring and summer-long Washington demonstration, Dr. King described it today as "a lobby-in against Congress." He called for "the honorable end" of a war in Vietnam that he said "has been made the excuse for evasion of domestic accord."

"We believe the highest patriotism demands the ending of that war and the opening of a bloodless war to final victory over racism and poverty," he said in a prepared statement.

"Flame throwers in Vietnam fan the flames in our cities," he said at another point in his statement. "I don't think the two matters can be separated, as some people continue to feel."

At a news conference in the, red brick education building of his Ebenezer Baptist Church, Dr. King told a handful of newsmen that members of the President's National Advisory Commission on Civil Disorders: "deserved the gratitude of the nation because they had both the wisdom to perceive the truth and the courage to state it" in their report, published in Washington last Saturday.

The commission's report declared that "white racism" was moving the United States toward two societies, "separate and unequal."

Dr. King said the commission's recommendations for legislation would be adopted as the basis of the demands the leadership of his demonstration will make public in about two weeks.

"It may be that in one or two instances we are stronger than they are," he said.

"The commission report," he also said, "is a physician's warning of approaching death [of American society], with a prescription to life. The duty of every American is to administer the remedy without regard for the cost and without delay."

During the two or three weeks of late April and early May, he said, 3,000 or more militant Negroes and whites will be streaming across the country on foot and in vehicles, toward Washington.

CARAVAN FROM MISSISSIPPI

On April 22, he said, he and a few leaders — perhaps no more than 30 — will begin the "educational phase" of the demonstration by calling formally on Administration and Congressional leaders. On the same day, a caravan that Dr. King termed a "mule train" of about 3,000 Negroes in wagons drawn by mules and horses, will start out for Washington from Mississippi.

The Mississippians and others who may join them may speed over thinly populated sections of the South by truck and bus, an official of the conference said later, but the "mule train" is to debouch for a slow transit on foot through Southern cities and sections of countryside.

Dr. King Plans Mass Protest in Capital June 15

BY BEN A. FRANKLIN | MARCH 30, 1968

GRENADA, MISS., MARCH 19 — The Rev. Dr. Martin Luther King Jr. said today he would summon to Washington on June 15 "a massive outpouring of hundreds of thousands of people, white and black" for a "special day of protest" in his "poor people's campaign" in the capital this spring and summer.

Dr. King disclosed the plan as he opened a three-week recruiting drive for marchers in his planned marathon demonstration "to upset Washington" in a demand for jobs or a guaranteed income for the nation's poor.

By car and by chartered airplane, Dr. King toured Mississippi counties that are among the poorest in the nation.

The Negro civil rights leader exhorted "whole families" of poor Delta Negroes to come to Washington during the week of April 22, when the demonstration there is scheduled to start, and "plague Congress, and the President until they do something."

This afternoon in the little Quitman County town of Marks in northwestern Mississippi, Dr. King said that he had been "deeply moved" and "made more determined than ever" by a visit to 100 cheerful but poorly dressed Negro children at what is somewhat loosely called the Marks Head Start Center.

The center, which has not received a single Federal antipoverty dollar under the preschool Head Start program in its two years of existence, is in the Eudora African Methodist Episcopal Zion Church, a shabby firetrap of a building whose interior walls are covered with funeral parlor calendars bearing gaudy pictures of a blond and ascetic-looking Christ.

For 20 minutes Dr. King stood silently at the pulpit and heard the impassioned pleas of Negro mothers for "shoes and a decent education" for their children.

"Johnson said when he come in he was going to wipe out poverty, ignorance and disease," one angry woman shouted. "Now where's our money?"

Then Dr. King responded.

"Even though Quitman County is the poorest in the United States, it's criminal for people to have to live in these conditions," he said. "I am very deeply touched. God does not want you to live like you are living."

Dr. King and a single carload of aides from his Southern Christian Leadership Conference met no white resistance on their daylong swing through an area of Mississippi where the civil rights organization has been active for several years.

In fact, one roughly dressed white man in Marks handed Dr. King a crisp $100 bill to help finance the Washington demonstration. He would not give his name.

The King party flew from here to Hattiesburg late tonight and is to tour southern Mississippi counties tomorrow, before turning east to Alabama and Georgia.

The Rev. Ralph D. Abernathy, vice president and treasurer of the leadership conference, drew a strong response today from 200 persons jammed into the Mount Zion Missionary Baptist Church in Batesville when he declared:

"We're going up there to talk to L.B.J., and if L.B.J. don't do something about what we tell him, we're going to put him down and get us another one that will."

Shift In Position Is Hinted By King: He Says He May Be Forced to Pick a Candidate

BY WALTER H. WAGGONER | MARCH 28, 1968

NEWARK, MARCH 27 — The Rev. Dr. Martin Luther King Jr. said today that the "crucial" nature of election issues at home and abroad might force him to abandon his customary nonpartisan stance and declare publicly for a Presidential candidate.

He described Senator Robert F. Kennedy and Senator Eugene J. McCarthy, both campaigning for the Democratic nomination, as "competent" men who offered an "alternative" to the "dead-end" policies of President Johnson.

However, Dr. King acknowledged that if the President were to negotiate an end to the war in Vietnam and "escalate the war on poverty at home" it was "very possible that those who are disenchanted with President Johnson could support him."

Asked whether he was disenchanted with the President, he replied, "very much so."

Dr. King made his comments at a news conference at Mount Calvary Missionary Baptist Church, which opened a daylong tour of the Negro slums, churches and schools in Newark and other North Jersey cities. He also visited the apartments of two Newark welfare families.

The tour is part of Dr. King's nationwide effort on behalf of the "Poor Peoples Campaign," which is to open with a demonstration in Washington on April 22.

Dr. King's first major visit to Newark — he has appeared here previously only for speaking engagements — began with an orderly meeting with members of the clergy at the Mount Calvary Missionary Baptist Church, an immaculate 10-year-old pink brick building of contemporary design in the South Ward.

He spoke privately to about 100 clergymen and friends who had waited from 10 A.M. to 11:25 for him to arrive from New York.

But Dr. King's biggest reception came at the predominantly Negro South Side High School, where he addressed a cheering, applauding crowd of about 1,400 students and teachers overflowing the auditorium.

He told his almost solidly Negro audience, which greeted him enthusiastically, that black people "must develop and maintain a continuing sense of somebodyness."

"Stand up with dignity and self-respect," he declared. "Too long black people have been ashamed of themselves. Now I'm black, but I'm black and beautiful."

There was a long outburst of applause, cheers and whistles.

Dr. King's visit, although hurried, spanned the extremes of Newark's social and economic spectrum. He had a private lunch with about 25 business and financial leaders at the New Jersey Bell Telephone Company, and later this afternoon he talked with LeRoi Jones, at the playwright's headquarters for the arts at 33 Sterling Street, known as Spirit House.

Mr. Jones, who is free on bail pending an appeal of his conviction on a weapons charge during the Newark riots last summer, said after the visit: "We talked about unifying the black people."

A tumultuous welcome by nearly 1,000 people awaited Dr. King when he arrived at 10 P.M. at the Abyssinian Baptist Church, 224 West Kinney Street, after he had visited churches in Paterson, Orange and Jersey City.

He was greeted with prolonged applause during his speech in the church when he asserted that the Government was spending $75 billion on an "evil unjust war."

He received a prolonged burst of cheers when he declared: "The hour has come for Newark, N. J., to have a black mayor."

Negro Is Killed In Memphis March

BY WALTER RUGABER | MARCH 29, 1967

MEMPHIS, TENN. MARCH 28 — A 16-year-old Negro youth was killed today in violence surrounding a massive protest march that was led through downtown Memphis by the Rev. Dr. Martin Luther King Jr.

A group of Negro youths smashed windows and looted stores as Dr. King led 6,000 demonstrators in support of the city's striking sanitation workers, most of them Negroes. Local leaders of the march halted the procession as the disorders continued.

As the march turned back, the police began using tear gas and chemical mace, an irritant, to clear the streets. A number of Negroes were affected by the gas and chemical mace and others were beaten with riot sticks wielded by the officers.

About 50 persons were injured but few were believed to have been seriously hurt. At least 120 persons were arrested throughout the day.

Gov. Buford Ellington called up 4,000 National Guard troops and a number of highway patrolmen at the request of Mayor Henry Loeb. A total of 8,000 more troops were placed on alert.

There was sporadic violence in the city before and after the march. The Memphis Transit Authority halted bus service this afternoon after three drivers were hurt and five vehicles were damaged in clashes.

The slain youth was identified as Larry Payne, 16 years old. A police official said he was shot when caught looting. The youth attacked a policeman with a butcher knife, the official source reported.

The Tennessee legislature hurriedly passed a law this afternoon giving cities the authority to set curfews, and Mayor Loeb imposed one beginning at 7 P.M. He also ordered all liquor stores closed for the day.

The police sealed off one block of Beale Street, where most of the rioting occurred, but otherwise traffic moved normally past the pawn shops and cheap stores that now dot the thoroughfare.

Placards, apparently dropped by the marchers, were scattered across the small park named for W. C. Handy, the famous jazz musician. A wreath in the park marked today as the 10th anniversary of his death.

Tonight, there were sporadic reports of isolated fires. But none of the blazes were reported to be serious, and many involved only garbage. There were no reports of mass movements in the Negro-community.

The Fire Department said it had received reports of 125 minor fires today. Since the sanitation strike began, however, the department has regularly received 50 to 75 calls a night as citizens angrily light piles of accumulated trash.

CONFLICTING REPORTS

Dr. King's march moved up Beale Street from the Clayborn Temple African Methodist Episcopal Church shortly after 11 A.M. The procession, headed for City Hall, halted just after turning onto Main Street.

There were conflicting accounts as to whether the youths blamed for the disorder darted out of the march or whether they were merely running along the sidewalks beside the procession.

The destruction that broke out at various points along the march is expected to raise more questions about Dr. King's projected crusade in Washington next month.

When he announced plans to begin a campaign of civil disobedience in the capital on April 22, he was closely questioned about the danger of violent forces infiltrating the ranks of his nonviolent protestors.

He acknowledged that the Washington drive was "risky" for this reason, but he said that his 3,000 demonstrators would be carefully trained in nonviolence and that destructive forces could be kept away from the activities of his group.

DR. KING LEAVES SCENE

Dr. King was whisked away from the march at the first sign of trouble. He was reportedly taken to a motel and could not be reached immediately. His office in Atlanta also declined to comment. The winner of the Nobel Peace Prize was said to be asleep early this evening, but an aide, the Rev. Bernard Lee, told reporters that Dr. King was "discouraged" by the disorders that broke out around the march.

"This incident has put us even more on our toes as to what some of the possibilities are," Mr. Lee said. He indicated that the Southern Christian Leadership Conference, which Dr. King heads, would rethink its planning for the Washington effort.

Mr. Lee said that the number of demonstration leaders for the Washington campaign would have to be increased from 1,000 to at least 2,000 and that more intensive training in nonviolent techniques would have to be administered.

Dr. King's aide said he was confident that if the protest here had been organized by the S.C.L.C. the violence could have been avoided. He was optimistic that the protest in Washington could be kept peaceful. As he departed, the police began firing tear gas at Negroes in the street. Witnesses said many of the marchers and bystanders were hit by the gas. Several were severely critical of the police for allegedly growing "panicky" and aiming indiscriminately.

"The cops did not attack the nucleus of the problem [the teen-agers responsible for the window breaking]," said James Ward, a bank executive and participant in the march. "They just started spraying tear gas everywhere."

It was apparent, however, that much of the window breaking and looting occurred just as the march passed along the streets. Some witnesses said rioters ran just ahead of the demonstrators.

Mr. Ward said, "I could hear the windows breaking as we came up the street, and as we passed the stores I saw apparel and other stuff scattered all over outside." He said he had not seen any looting, however.

The police moved in on stragglers with clubs and pounded many into submission. Some of the Negroes fought back in more or less isolated encounters, hurling bricks and bottles. A number of policemen were hurt.

More than 1,300 of the city's sanitation workers went on strike Feb. 12, asking for higher pay, union recognition and a union dues check-off.

The city maintained partial sanitation service by using strikebreakers and supervisory employees.

The strike by the mostly Negro garbage collectors polarized the racism in this city of 550,000 on the east bank of the Mississippi River. About 40 per cent of the population is Negro.

A SYMBOL OF GRIEVANCES

For many of them, the sanitation walkout is a symbol of deeper grievances. The Southern Regional Council, a biracial organization that concentrates on research and publication in the race relations field, said in a report issued Sunday:

"Mayor Loeb's handling of the sanitation strike, with concurrence of the City Council, apparently triggered the release in the Negro community of built-up resentment over low wages generally and underemployment of Negroes in the local government."

Efforts to settle the strike appear stalled. Mr. Loeb has been severely criticized for his role in the dispute, particularly for his refusal to recognize the union. Whites, however, seem to back the Mayor solidly.

The sanitation workers now earn an average of $1.70 an hour. They sought a 15-cent an hour increase, while Mayor Loeb offered 8 cents.

Court Bars March in Memphis; Dr. King Calls Order 'Illegal'

BY EARL CALDWELL | APRIL 4, 1968

MEMPHIS, APRIL 3 — A Federal court order was issued here today prohibiting the Rev. Dr. Martin Luther King Jr. from leading a civil rights protest in Memphis on Monday.

Dr. King, in a determined and angry mood, promptly called the order "illegal and unconstitutional" and said that there was a "real possibility" that he would not obey it.

After hearing arguments from City Attorney Frank Gianotti, United States District Court Judge Bailey Brown issued the temporary restraining order.

Originally, Dr. King had planned his demonstration for Friday but after meeting with local leaders this morning, the march was postponed until Monday.

The demonstration was planned in support of the city's 1,300 sanitation workers, who walked off their jobs Feb. 12 in a dispute over wages, union recognition and a dues checkoff arrangement.

'FAR BEYOND A MARCH'

But Dr. King said that the protest had taken on significance "far beyond a march now." He said that his organization, the Southern Christian Leadership Conference, was going "all out to deal with this Memphis problem."

About 90 per cent of the sanitation men here are Negroes and the strike has divided much of this city of 550,000 along racial lines. The population is 40 per cent Negro.

Dr. King explained that the march had been put off until Monday in order to give union men from across the country time to come here and join in the protest. Dr. King said that he expected about 5,000 men from other cities to travel here and join the protest.

In addition to the protest scheduled for Monday, Dr. King also said that arrangements were being made "to go all out" in putting economic pressure on the city through various boycotts.

"Up until now," he said, "only the sanitation men have felt the pain of this. We plan to redistribute the pain."

Dr. King became involved in the dispute when he came here last Thursday to lead a march in support of the workers. That demonstration, which started out as a peaceful protest, ended in violence that took the life of a 16-year-old Negro youth.

In an effort to prevent further demonstrations while tensions remained high in the city, Mayor Henry Loeb instructed Mr. Gianotti to seek the Federal injunction that was granted by Justice Brown.

Accepting the city's argument that another march was likely to cause "great damage," Justice Brown not only imposed restraining orders on Dr. King but also on all persons under his authority and those acting in concert with him.

Although he said that he might defy the court order, Dr. King said that he would first attempt to have it set aside in the courts. He said that his lawyers would go into Federal Court tomorrow in an effort to have the order dissolved. If this fails, he continued, his lawyers will attempt to have the order upset in the United States Court of Appeals.

"Beyond that," Dr. King said, "it is a matter of conscience. It will be on the basis of my conscience saying that we have a moral right and responsibility to march."

The civil rights leader, speaking from his hotel room after a mid-afternoon meeting with his lawyers, recalled that he had been forced to defy court orders in the past. He said that he had spent a week in jail in Alabama late last year as the result of having defied a court injunction in Birmingham back in 1963.

CHAPTER 5

'Martin Luther King Is Slain in Memphis'

Under the banner headline above, The New York Times published 26 articles about Dr. King's murder and the reactions to it. Dr. King had known his life was at risk — he had been threatened, stabbed and shot at. But he believed firmly that it was a risk worth taking to fight the racism that stubbornly persisted in the United States. Dr. King met with success — The Fair Housing Act, for which he had heavily advocated, was passed the day after his funeral — but recognized that there was much work still to be done.

Guard Called Out; Curfew Is Ordered in Memphis, but Fires and Looting Erupt

BY EARL CALDWELL | APRIL 5, 1968

MEMPHIS, FRIDAY, APRIL 5 — The Rev. Dr. Martin Luther King Jr., who preached nonviolence and racial brotherhood, was fatally shot here last night by a distant gunman who then raced away and escaped.

Four thousand National Guard troops were ordered into Memphis by Gov. Buford Ellington after the 39-year-old Nobel Prize-winning civil rights leader died.

A curfew was imposed on the shocked city of 550,000 inhabitants, 40 per cent of whom are Negro.

But the police said the tragedy had been followed by incidents that included sporadic shooting, fires, bricks and bottles thrown at policemen, and looting that started in Negro districts and then spread over the city.

WHITE CAR SOUGHT

Police Director Frank Holloman said the assassin might have been a white man who was "50 to 100 yards away, in a flophouse."

Chief of Detectives W. P. Huston said a late model white Mustang was believed to have been the killer's getaway car. Its occupant was described as a bareheaded white man in his 30's, wearing a black suit and black tie.

The detective chief said the police had chased two cars near the motel where Dr. King was shot and had halted one that had two out-of-town men as occupants. The men were questioned but seemed to have nothing to do with the killing, he said.

RIFLE FOUND NEARBY

A high-powered 30.06-caliber rifle was found about a block from the scene of the shooting, on South Main Street "We think it's the gun," Chief Huston said, reporting it would be turned over to the Federal Bureau of Investigation.

Dr. King was shot while he leaned over a second-floor railing outside his room at the Lorraine Motel. He was chatting with two friends just before starting for dinner.

One of the friends was a musician, and Dr. King had just asked him to play a Negro spiritual, "Precious Lord, Take My Hand," at a rally that was to have been held two hours later in support of striking Memphis sanitation men.

Paul Hess, assistant administrator at St. Joseph's Hospital, where Dr. King died despite emergency surgery, said the minister had "received a gunshot wound on the right side of the neck, at the root of the neck, a gaping wound."

"He was pronounced dead at 7:05 P.M. Central standard time (8:05 P.M. New York time) by staff doctors," Mr. Hess said. "They did everything humanly possible."

Dr. King's mourning associates sought to calm the people they met by recalling his messages of peace, but there was widespread concern by law enforcement officers here and elsewhere over potential reactions.

In a television broadcast after the curfew was ordered here, Mr. Holloman said, "rioting has broken out in parts of the city" and "looting is rampant."

Dr. King had come back to Memphis Wednesday morning to organize support once again for 1,300 sanitation workers who have been striking since Lincoln's Birthday. Just a week ago yesterday he led a march in the strikers' cause that ended in violence. A 16-year-old Negro was killed, 62 persons were injured and 200 were arrested.

Yesterday Dr. King had been in his second-floor room — Number 306 — throughout the day. Just about 6 P.M. he emerged, wearing a silkish-looking black suit and white shirt.

Solomon Jones Jr., his driver, had been waiting to take him by car to the home of the Rev. Samuel Kyles of Memphis for dinner. Mr. Jones said later he had observed, "It's cold outside, put your topcoat on," and Dr. King had replied, "O. K., I will."

TWO MEN IN COURTYARD

Dr. King, an open-faced, genial man, leaned over a green iron railing to chat with an associate, Jesse Jackson, standing just below him in a courtyard parking lot.

"Do you know Ben?" Mr. Jackson asked, introducing Ben Branch of Chicago, a musician who was to play at the night's rally.

"Yes, that's my man!" Dr. King glowed.

The two men recalled Dr. King's asking for the playing of the spiritual. "I really want you to play that tonight," Dr. King said, enthusiastically.

The Rev. Ralph W. Abernathy, perhaps Dr. King's closest friend, was just about to come out of the motel room when the sudden loud noise burst out.

Dr. King toppled to the concrete second-floor walkway. Blood gushed from the right jaw and neck area. His necktie had been ripped off by the blast.

"He had just bent over," Mr. Jackson recalled later. "If he had been standing up, he wouldn't have been hit in the face."

POLICEMEN 'ALL OVER'

"When I turned around," Mr. Jackson went on, bitterly, "I saw police coming from everywhere. They said, 'where did it come from?' And I said, 'behind you.' The police were coming from where the shot came."

Mr. Branch asserted that the shot had come from "the hill on the other side of the street."

"When I looked up, the police and the sheriff's deputies were running all around," Mr. Branch declared.

"We didn't need to call the police," Mr. Jackson said. "They were here all over the place."

Mr. Kyles said Dr. King had stood in the open "about three minutes."

Mr. Jones, the driver, said that a squad car with four policemen in it drove down the street only moments before the gunshot. The police had been circulating throughout the motel area on precautionary patrols.

After the shot, Mr. Jones said, he saw a man "with something white on his face" creep away from a thicket across the street.

Someone rushed up with a towel to stem the flow of Dr. King's blood. Mr. Kyles said he put a blanket over Dr. King, but "I knew he was gone." He ran down the stairs and tried to telephone from the motel office for an ambulance.

Mr. Abernathy hurried up with a second larger towel.

POLICE WITH HELMETS

Policemen were pouring into the motel area, carrying rifles and shotguns and wearing riot helmets. But the King aides said it seemed to be 10 or 15 minutes before a Fire Department ambulance arrived.

Dr. King was apparently still living when he reached the St. Joseph's Hospital operating room for emergency surgery. He was borne in on a stretcher, the bloody towel over his head.

It was the same emergency room to which James H. Meredith, first Negro enrolled at the University of Mississippi, was taken after he was ambushed and shot in June 1965, at Hernando, Miss., a few miles south of Memphis. Mr. Meredith was not seriously hurt.

Outside the emergency room some of Dr. King's aides waited in forlorn hope. One was Chauncey Eskridge, his legal adviser. He broke into sobs when Dr. King's death was announced.

"A man full of life, full of love and he was shot," Mr. Eskridge said. "He had always lived with that expectation — but nobody ever expected it to happen."

But the Rev. Andrew Young, executive director of Dr. King's Southern Christian Leadership Conference, recalled there had been some talk Wednesday night about possible harm to Dr. King in Memphis.

Mr. Young recalled: "He said he had reached the pinnacle of fulfillment with his nonviolent movement, and these reports did not bother him."

Mr. Young believed that the fatal shot might have been fired from a passing car. "It sounded like a firecracker," he said.

In a nearby building, a newsman who had been watching a television program thought, however, that "it was a tremendous blast that sounded like a bomb."

There were perhaps 15 persons in the motel courtyard area when Dr. King was shot, all believed to be Negroes and Dr. King's associates.

Past the courtyard is a small empty swimming pool. Then comes Mulberry Street, a short street only three blocks away from storied Beale Street on the fringe of downtown Memphis.

FIRE STATION NEARBY

On the other side of the street is a six-foot-brick restraining wall, with bushes and grass atop it and a hillside going on to a patch of trees.

Behind the trees is a rusty wire fence enclosing backyards of two-story brick and frame houses. At the corner at Butler Street is a newish-looking white brick fire station.

Police were reported to have chased a late-model blue or white car through Memphis and north to Millington. A civilian in another car that had a citizens band radio was also reported to have pursued the fleeing car and to have opened fire on it.

The police first cordoned off an area of about five blocks around the Lorraine Motel, chosen by Dr. King for his stay here because it is Negro-owned. The two-story motel is an addition to a small two-story hotel in a largely Negro area.

Mayor Henry Loeb had ordered a curfew here after last week's disorder, and National Guard units had been on duty for five days until they were deactivated Wednesday.

Last night the Mayor reinstated the curfew at 6:35 and declared: "After the tragedy which has happened in Memphis tonight, for the protection of all our citizens, we are putting the curfew back in effect. All movement is restricted except for health or emergency reasons."

Governor Ellington, calling out the National Guard and pledging all necessary action by the state to prevent disorder, announced:

"For the second time in recent days, I most earnestly ask the people of Memphis and Shelby County to remain calm.

"I do so again tonight in the face of this most regrettable incident.

"Every possible action is being taken to apprehend the person or persons responsible for committing this act.

"We are also taking precautionary steps to prevent any acts of disorder. I can fully appreciate the feelings and emotions which this crime has aroused, but for the benefit of everyone, all of our citizens must exercise restraint, caution and good judgment."

National Guard planes flew over the state to bring in contingents of riot-trained highway patrolmen. Units of the Arkansas State Patrol were deputized and brought into Memphis.

Assistant Chief Bartholomew early this morning said that unidentified persons had shot from rooftops and windows at policemen eight or 10 times. He said bullets had shattered one police car's windshield, wounding two policemen with flying glass. They were treated at the same hospital where Dr. King died.

Sixty arrests were made for looting, burglary and disorderly conduct, chief Bartholomew said.

Numerous minor injuries were reported in four hours of clashes between civilians and law enforcement officers. But any serious disorders were under control by 11:15 P.M., Chief Bartholomew said. Early this morning streets were virtually empty except for patrol cars riding without headlights on.

ONCE STABBED IN HARLEM

In his career Dr. King had suffered beatings and blows. Once — on Sept. 20, 1958 — he was stabbed in a Harlem department store in New York by a Negro woman later adjudged insane.

That time he underwent a four-hour operation to remove a steel letter opener that had been plunged into his upper left chest. For a time he was on the critical list, but he told his wife, while in the hospital, "I don't hold any bitterness toward this woman."

In Memphis, Dr. King's chief associates met in his room after he died. They included Mr. Young, Mr. Abernathy, Mr. Jackson, the Rev. James Bevel and Hosea Williams.

They had to step across a drying pool of Dr. King's blood to enter. Someone had thrown a crumpled pack of cigarettes into the blood.

After 15 minutes they emerged. Mr. Jackson looked at the blood. He embraced Mr. Abernathy.

"Stand tall!" somebody exhorted.

"Murder! Murder!" Mr. Bevel groaned. "Doc said that's not the way."

"Doc" was what they often called Dr. King.

Then the murdered leader's aides said they would go on to the hall where tonight's rally was to have been held. They wanted to urge calm upon the mourners. Some policemen sought to dissuade them. But eventually the group did start out, with a police escort.

At the Federal Bureau of Investigation office here, Robert Jensen, special agent in charge, said the F. B. I. had entered the murder investigation at the request of Attorney General Ramsey Clark.

Last night Dr. King's body was taken to the Shelby County morgue, according to the police. They said it would be up to Dr. Derry Francisco, county medical examiner, to order further disposition.

The Lone Journalist on the Scene When King Was Shot and the Newsroom He Rallied

BY DAVID MARGOLICK | APRIL 3, 2018

EARL CALDWELL wrote history on the night of April 4, 1968, when he reported firsthand on the assassination of Martin Luther King Jr. for The New York Times. But he made history right before that, when he became the first black reporter The Times had assigned to follow the civil rights leader.

That night, Caldwell spearheaded the dozens of reporters, editors and photographers hastily assembled for the story — an additional first for a black journalist and, in a larger sense, another result of the campaign for greater black inclusion in American life that King had come to personify over the previous 13 years.

The milestones in King's career — the Montgomery bus boycott, the protests in Birmingham, the marches on Washington and from Selma to Montgomery — had always been the province of white correspondents, principally native Southerners (Claude Sitton, Roy Reed, Gene Roberts and John Herbers, among them) steeped in racial matters for whom the major stops on the civil rights itinerary represented home turf. But that changed when King, in Memphis to support striking local sanitation workers, and Caldwell, there to follow him around, each checked into the Lorraine Motel on April 3.

Also always left to white reporters was the task of writing, and periodically updating, King's obituary. The paper first prepared one in 1960, when King was all of 31 years old. Only the dateline and the lead paragraph, detailing the circumstances of his demise, were omitted.

In this sense, The Times and King were congruent long before April 4, 1968: Each had anticipated his early, and violent, death.

HERE'S A LOOK at what happened inside and outside our newsroom that night, and in the days after — including a first-person account from Earl Caldwell, who is currently an assistant professor at the Scripps Howard School of Journalism and Communications at Hampton University in Hampton, Va. He declined to comment for this piece. The longer article from which it is excerpted, titled "7 Days That Shook the World and The Times" — written, without a byline, for an internal April 1968 Times publication, Times Talk — began with our coverage of President Lyndon B. Johnson's surprise announcement, that same week, that he would not seek re-election.

The tumult that shook the nation early in April kept Times crews at high boil for a full week. The president announced he would not run, Martin Luther King was assassinated and violence erupted across the country. Even the oldest hands on the paper could recall no period to equal it.

AT 7:10 ON Thursday evening, April 4, [the national news editor Claude] Sitton's phone rang. It was Earl Caldwell, calling from Memphis. "King's been shot," he reported breathlessly.

"Who?" Sitton asked.

"King. Martin Luther King."

"How serious?" Sitton asked.

Caldwell didn't know, but told Sitton, "It looks bad."

He had gone to Memphis the day before to cover Dr. King's march for the striking sanitation men. Here's his account of what happened, as written for Times Talk.

> *It didn't have the sharp crack of a rifle shot. It was more of a blast, like a giant firecracker or a bomb.*
>
> *In Memphis, it was near 6 p.m. The Huntley-Brinkley news show had just finished on TV. My room, No. 215, was on the ground floor of the motel, just under the balcony where the Rev. Dr. Martin Luther King Jr. was standing and talking when the shot rang out. The phone service at the motel was poor and I'd been stalking about the room, waiting for a line to phone New York an insert on the story I'd been working on.*

It was warm in the room and I cracked the door and then, restless and angry that I was missing the deadline because of the phone, I took off my shoes and trousers. A short while earlier a coke bottle had fallen off the balcony and broken just outside the window of my room. For some reason I had been jumpy when the bottle fell. I ran to the door, thinking it was a shot or something.

Then came the blast. Before any commotion or before I heard anything I knew that something was wrong and went for the door that was still partially opened.

I saw people jumping around in the courtyard in front of the balcony. My first thought was that someone had set off a firecracker. "Man, what a lousy joke," I thought at first. Then the events began to close in.

This car, it raced across the black-top yard [which was also a parking lot] toward my room and then stopped and went back and then lurched forward again. It stopped again and the Negro man sitting inside at the wheel was rocking back and forth with his hands at his head now and screaming "Oh no, oh no, oh no." I yelled at him: "What's the matter? What's the matter? What's going on?" But he never answered or before he could someone else was yelling: "They shot him. They shot him."

JOSEPH LOUW/THE LIFE IMAGES COLLECTION/GETTY IMAGES

Earl Caldwell (standing next to police officer) on the balcony of the Lorraine Motel as Martin Luther King Jr. lies mortally wounded. Caldwell's room was one floor below. He raced up after he heard the shot.

I dashed out into the lot but a few steps outside the door I remembered my trousers. I don't know why but I knew it was Dr. King. I started back for my pants but stopped and ran out again. Then back into the room where I grabbed my pants and slipped on my shoes without bothering to lace them up. On the way out I grabbed a stack of copy paper, a pen and my raincoat. Later, I wondered why the raincoat but as it turned out, it was a good move. When I ran out the last time, I forgot my room key and locked myself out into what was to become a very chilly night.

I ran into the lot and remember seeing James Bevel, a member of Dr. King's executive staff crouching near the balcony. I ran closer and then I got down, too, but I could see Dr. King lying up there on the balcony. I jumped up and then back down and then up and down again as the others did too. It dawned on me at some point that I was doing this along with everyone else because there might be another shot.

And then, someone was on the balcony. It was Abernathy, the Rev. Ralph D. Abernathy, Dr. King's close friend and long-time aide. Then someone else was on the balcony and I ran over to the stairs and went up too. Abernathy was holding Dr. King about his head and leaning over him as though he were trying to talk with him. The blood. The wound was as big as your fist. His eyes. They were open but they had such a strange look. Eyes that were not seeing anything. I thought he was unconscious.

"Write. Write, write down everything you see," I thought. I began to jot down on paper who was there, what they were doing, time, what they were saying. "Get it all down, get it all down," and then a second thought: phone. Call the office, call the office I kept thinking. I hustled down the stairs and started for my room but about half-way I remembered that the phones were busy. I remembered one at the other end of the motel and I started to run in that direction.

Suddenly there were all of these police with shotguns and unholstered pistols and they seemed to be coming from across the street, from the direction where the shot had been fired. I remember a cop coming up to me grabbing my arm and asking which way did the shot come from. "Across the street, I think. Over there. I don't know. I don't know."

Again I remembered the phone and started to run in that direction. Change. A dime. I had two nickels in my pocket. I felt out of breath but I remember methodically calling the operator. "I'd like to make a credit card call to New York ... area code 212-556-7356. Martha." Martha answered. "Martha, I'd like to speak to Claude, it's an emergency.

Claude answered quickly but when he did I couldn't talk. All of a sudden, I was out of breath. Finally I blurted it out. "King's been shot."

Sitton told him to get further details and call back. He hung up, called over to [the metropolitan editor Arthur] Gelb, "King's been shot," and hurried to the news desk. It was a full 10 minutes before the wire services moved the bulletins about the shooting. And even then no one knew how serious it was.

The metropolitan staff was winding up an exhausting day which had seen the installation of Archbishop Cooke and the president's visit to New York. The last stories were crossing the desk. Gelb immediately collared Peter Kihss, told him to be prepared to write a first-edition story on Dr. King if Caldwell was unable to file. Tony Lukas was finishing a story about the president's day in New York. He was instructed to go at once to Memphis. Martha Moraghan, national desk secretary, had called American Airlines, learned there was a 7:50 plane out of La Guardia Airport. Sitton had cajoled an airline executive into holding it until Lukas could get there.

Murray Schumach, who had just finished a piece on the city's security arrangements during the president's visit, was ready to go home. Gelb stopped him. Murray had written an advance obit on Dr King a year and a half ago. It was in type in the composing room. Gelb asked him to update and revise it.

At 7:30 (New York time; it was an hour earlier in Memphis) Caldwell called back. He told Sitton that King had been taken to a hospital, but he didn't know which one. Gelb put four rewrite men on the phones to try and find out. They called Memphis hospitals, police, newspapers. A few minutes after 8, Mike Kaufman broke off a phone conversation to call to Gelb: "King died at 6:12. I have it from The Memphis Commercial Appeal."

At the news desk Assistant Managing Editor Ted Bernstein and News Editor Lew Jordan had laid out the front page by 6:30. Max Frankel's piece on the president's upcoming trip to Hawaii was to lead the paper. The installation of the archbishop was to be the off-lead, illustrated with two four-column cuts of the service. They quickly prepared an alternate dummy. The Johnson story was moved to column five and space was made for a three-column head on the King story. A two-column cut of Dr. King was rushed through photoengraving.

Kihss was taking Caldwell's eyewitness account on the phone, skillfully weaving into the story all the vital information he had assembled in the few minutes before Sitton switched Caldwell's second call to him. Together they put together a two-column story, full of vivid dialogue and descriptions of the scene on the motel balcony. A new lead from Frankel updated his Johnson story to include the president's decision to postpone his trip. [The editorial page editor] John Oakes was dining in a restaurant when the death flash came. Ralph Chodes, who makes up the editorial page, called him. Oakes wrote a few sentences on the back of a menu and called it in for the first edition. After dinner, at home, he expanded it for later editions.

Make-up Editor Dave Lidman and his assistants had rearranged inside pages to make room for the Caldwell story and for Schumach's four-column obit. (Next day readers wondered how The Times could be on the street so quickly with a full-length obituary. Advance obits of important people are kept in type for just such emergencies.)

Sitton had been on the phone since the first word of the shooting came in. He called B.D. Ayres on the night desk in the Washington bureau and asked him to find out what the Justice Department was doing about the shooting. He alerted his Southern regional correspondents Martin Waldron in Austin, Walter Rugaber in Atlanta, Tony Ripley in Tampa. When word of the death came through, he sent Waldron to Memphis, Ripley to Atlanta to join Rugaber.

Lukas and Waldron met head-on in front of The Memphis Commercial Appeal office about 10 p.m. Lukas had arrived from New York; Waldron from Texas. They tried to call 43rd Street. No calls were allowed out, the operator informed them, unless it was a matter of life or death. "It is," Lukas told her. "My editor will kill me if I don't get through." It didn't work. About 11 o'clock, suspecting that the men in Memphis were having trouble getting through, Gelb had Bob McFadden on rewrite call them at the Commercial Appeal. They kept the line open several hours, dictating stuff they had picked up about the situation in Memphis. It was incorporated in a roundup written in the office by Syl Fox.

Anticipating riots but not knowing where they might break out, Sitton reached his Midwest correspondents — Doug Kneeland in Lincoln, Neb., Don Janson in Indianapolis — and got them to Chicago. He wanted them close to a big airport ready to move out quickly wherever they might be needed. As violence flared throughout the week, Kneeland flew to Pittsburgh, Cincinnati and Kansas City; Janson stayed in Chicago to cover the disturbances there.

Arthur Gelb held all his men and called in others. He put some on the telephones to get reaction from civil rights and political leaders. He assigned others to background pieces. It was Sunday night [when Johnson unexpectedly announced he would not seek re-election] all over again, only more so. As reports of looting and disturbances came in, Gelb sent men scurrying to trouble spots — Gerry Fraser and John Kifner, accompanied by Photographer Don Charles, to Harlem; Rudy Johnson to Bedford-Stuyvesant; Steve Roberts into Midtown. Tom Johnson took their reports as they called in, put together a front-page story for late editions. Larry Van Gelder rounded up a reaction story. Fraser, Kifner and Charles stayed through the night in Harlem, where the situation worsened after the paper had closed. They assembled good material and pictures for the next day's paper.

Washington staffers, with an old-fashioned police story on their hands (unlike the calm abstractions of their accustomed beats), worked without let-up on the riots that broke out in the capital on Thursday night and kept the city under curfew through the weekend. Carl Spriggs, a news clerk, went to the heart of the violence Thursday night, got within arm's length of Stokely Carmichael and got an exclusive report on his inflammatory remarks about guns. All that night and through the weekend he roamed the streets amid the violence, as did John Finney, Ben Welles and Fred Graham. Graham got tear-gassed. Maggie Hunter and Eileen Shanahan pitched in as rewrite men. As one of the few Washington natives in the bureau, Eileen also monitored the police radio and helped out on the geography of the city. Dave Brewster, assistant librarian, did leg work at the police station. Barbara Dubivsky, Sunday department representative; John Sterba, Scotty Reston's assistant, and Diane Henry, news assistant, manned the telephones as the men called in.

Bob Phelps pulled things together; Hal Gal, assistant news editor, and Ayres practically never left the desk during the weekend. In a corner of the bureau, Ben Franklin, Middle Atlantic correspondent, wove the material together. Norris Kealey and his wire room crew sent it catapulting to New York, where the national copy desk, with Ray O'Neill and Art Reed in charge, took over.

The late editions of the April 5 Times, under a banner head, carried 15 separate stories relating to Dr. King and eight photographs. Again, advertising was jettisoned to make room for it all. Archbishop Cooke conducted a steady retreat through the night, ended up at the bottom of Page 1. Distribution through the week held to over 1,000,000 copies.

The pressures on the local and national staffs seemed as if they would never let up — disorders, official mourning, the march in Memphis, the funeral in Atlanta. Sitton and Gelb played a complicated chess game with their men, moved them around the country, around the city as events dictated. The Times had a crew of nine in Atlanta on April 9, the day of the funeral, more than most states had representatives. Rugaber and Ripley were joined by Caldwell and Lukas, who came from Memphis, and by Homer Bigart, John Kifner, Ted Fiske, Deirdre Carmody and Don Charles, who flew down from New York.

By the time it was all over, editors, reporters, rewrite men and desk men had the twitches. The general air was "What next?"

DAVID MARGOLICK, A FORMER REPORTER FOR THE NEW YORK TIMES, IS A CONTRIBUTING EDITOR AT VANITY FAIR. HIS LATEST BOOK, "THE PROMISE AND THE DREAM: THE UNTOLD STORY OF MARTIN LUTHER KING, JR. AND ROBERT F. KENNEDY," WAS PUBLISHED ON APRIL 3, 2018.

Dismay In Nation; Negroes Urge Others to Carry on Spirit of Nonviolence

BY LAWRENCE VAN GELDER | APRIL 5, 1968

DISMAY, SHAME, ANGER and foreboding marked the nation's reaction last night to the Rev. Martin Luther King Jr.'s murder.

From the high offices of state to the man in the street, news of the moderate civil rights leader's violent death in Memphis yesterday drew, for the most part, stunned and sober statements.

Most major Negro organizations and Negro leaders, lamenting Dr. King's death, expressed hope that it serve as a spur to others to carry on in his spirit of nonviolence. But some Negro militants responded with bitterness and anger.

Roy Wilkins, executive director of the National Association for the Advancement of Colored People, said his organization was "shocked and deeply grieved by the dastardly murder of Dr. Martin Luther King."

"His murderer or murderers must be promptly apprehended and brought to justice," Mr. Wilkins said.

'A MAN OF PEACE'

"Dr. King was a symbol of the nonviolent civil rights protest movement. He was a man of peace, of dedication, of great courage. His senseless assassination solves nothing. It will not stay the civil rights movement; it will instead spur it to greater activity."

Whitney M. Young Jr., executive director of the National Urban League, said, "We are unspeakably shocked by the murder of Martin Luther King, one of the greatest leaders of our time. This is a bitter reflection on America. We fear for our country.

"The only possible answer now is for the nation to act immediately on what Dr. King has been fighting for — passage of the civil rights and anti-poverty bills and a true and just equality for all men. Those of us who have remained loyal to his concept of nonviolence have been dealt a mortal blow."

Mayor Richard G. Hatcher of Gary, Ind., a Negro, termed the death of Dr. King "every man's loss."

"Men who care for humankind and struggle for its salvation through reason and faith have lost a leader of monumental stature," he said. "A man of his magnitude will not soon pass this way again."

At his home in Stamford, Conn., the former baseball star Jackie Robinson called the shooting "the most disturbing and distressing thing we've had to face in a long time."

Dr. Kenneth B. Clark, a Negro who is a psychologist and head of the Metropolitan Applied Research Center, said in a faltering voice: "You have to cry out in anguish for this country … weep for this country."

In Los Angeles, Negro leaders quickly expressed hope that community sentiment would be keyed to the nonviolence for which Dr. King crusaded rather than to the harsh circumstances of his death.

"I hope the people of the United States and especially of Los Angeles will keep a cool head and a calm spirit and let the law take its course," said Gilbert Lindsay, one of three Negroes on the 15-member City Council.

Sen. Edward W. Brooke, Republican of Massachusetts, a Negro declared: "In our anguish and bitterness of this awful event, we must not lose sight of the meaning of this great man's life. The vindication of Dr. King's historic endeavors can only come through our renewed dedication to the human goals of brotherly love and equal justice which he so nobly advanced."

William Booth, chairman of New York City's Commission on Human Rights, said, "I would hope that no one would use Dr. King's death as an excuse for further violence."

Another call for restraint came from James Farmer, former national director of the Congress of Racial Equality, who said:

"Every racist in the country has killed Dr. King. Evil societies always destroy their consciences. The only fitting memorial to this martyred leader is a monumental commitment — now, not a day later — to eliminate racism. Dr. King hated bloodshed. His own blood must not now trigger more bloodshed."

ANGRY RESPONSE

An angry reaction came in Washington from Julius Hobson, a Negro who heads a militant but nonviolent civil rights group called ACT. Mr. Hobson said, "The next black man who comes into the black community preaching nonviolence should be violently dealt with by the black people who hear him. The Martin Luther King concept of nonviolence died with him. It was a foreign ideology anyway — as foreign to this violent country as speaking Russian."

Another bitter reaction came from Lincoln O. Lynch, the former associate national director of CORE and chairman of the United Black Front. He said, "The assassination of Martin Luther King, in my opinion, will begin to wake up black people to the fact that it is imperative to abandon the unconditional nonviolent concept expounded by Dr. King and adopt a position that for every Martin Luther King who falls, 10 white racists will go down with him. There is no other way. White America understands no other language."

The Most Rev. Terence J. Cooke, who was installed yesterday as the Roman Catholic Archbishop of New York, knelt in prayer with Archbishop Iakovos, the Greek Orthodox primate of North and South America, at a reception at the Greek Orthodox headquarters at 10 East 97th Street.

Side by side, kneeling on a red-carpeted stair before the Byzantine altar, the two prelates said the Lord's Prayer, and then Archbishop Cooke delivered a prayer for himself and Archbishop Iakovos:

"Dear Lord," he said, "we ask you to receive the soul of Martin Luther King, who in his days did so much to give leadership, to justice for all. We pray the ideals he struggled for, the ideals he gave his life for, will be realized, so that soon America will be one, at peace, where liberty is given to all."

Senator Jacob K. Javits said Dr. King's death "demands of all of us restraint and understanding and a renewed dedication to carry on the work of justice and decency among men of all races — the cause for which Dr. Martin Luther King gave his life. His doctrine of nonviolence will overcome, as he planned it should."

Former Vice President Richard M. Nixon called upon all Americans "to try in a new spirit of reconciliation to redeem this terrible act."

Mr. Nixon told newsmen he was canceling scheduled campaign appearances today and tomorrow in Minnesota because of Dr. King's death.

Telegrams of sympathy were sent to Mrs. King by Ambassador to the United Nations Arthur J. Goldberg and by Dr. Ralph J. Bunche, Under Secretary for Special Political Affairs of the United Nations.

Dr. Bunche, who is a Negro, said the assault on Dr. King "inevitably will be a most grievous blow to the cause of racial harmony throughout this country."

In Texas, Gov. John B. Connally Jr., who was wounded by a sniper when President Kenny was assassinated, said Dr. King had "contributed much to the chaos and turbulence in this country, but he did not deserve this fate."

He said the murder was an act "which tends to crumble away our society."

WALLACE'S VIEW

George C. Wallace, former Governor of Alabama, a segregationist candidate for President, called the assassination of Dr. King a "senseless, regrettable act."

Statements of grief at the death of Dr. King were issued by Rabbi Philip Rudin, president of the Synagogue Council of America; the Right Rev. Horace W. B. Donegan, Episcopal Bishop of New York, and Rabbi Arthur J. Lelyveld, president of the American Jewish Congress.

Expression of grief came also from Morris B. Abram, president of the American Jewish Committee; the Right Rev. John E. Hines, Presiding Bishop of the Episcopal Church; Dr. Sterling W. Brown, president of the National Conference of Christians and Jews; the Rev. Dr. Dan M. Potter, executive secretary of the Protestant Council of the city of New York, and Dr. R. H. Edwin Espy, general secretary of the National Council of Churches.

In Milwaukee, the Rev. James Groppi, the white Roman Catholic priest who has led the city's open housing marches, said: "This is certainly not going to be conducive to peaceful racial relations."

In Brisbane, Australia, the evangelist Billy Graham said the slaying indicated that "tens of thousands of Americans are mentally deranged."

"It indicates the sickness of the American society and is going to further inflame passions and hates," he said.

President's Plea

BY THE NEW YORK TIMES | APRIL 5, 1968

WASHINGTON, APRIL 4 — President Johnson deplored tonight in a brief television address to the nation the "brutal slaying" of the Rev. Dr. Martin Luther King Jr.

He asked "every citizen to reject the blind violence that has struck Dr. King, who lived by nonviolence." Mr. Johnson said he was postponing his scheduled departure tonight for a Honolulu conference on Vietnam and that instead he would leave tomorrow.

The President spoke from the White House. At the Washington Hilton Hotel, where Democratic members of Congress had gathered to honor the President and the Vice President, Mr. Humphrey, his voice strained with emotion, said:

"Martin Luther King stands with our other American martyrs in the cause of freedom and justice. His death is a terrible tragedy."

The dinner was canceled 10 to 15 minutes after the Vice President spoke. Mr. Johnson, who was scheduled to appear at the dinner, canceled his plans to attend.

F.B.I. INQUIRY ORDERED

Attorney General Ramsey Clark ordered an immediate inquiry by the Federal Bureau of Investigation into the shooting of Dr. King in Memphis.

He said the purpose of the investigation would be to determine whether any Federal law had been violated.

One provision of the law that could be invoked makes it a crime to engage in a conspiracy to deprive a person of his civil rights.

In addition to F.B.I. agents, Department of Justice civil rights representatives were on the scene in Memphis and were in touch with the Attorney General.

Military sources said that no National Guard units had yet been Federalized and no Regular Army troops had been alerted yet for possible movement to cities where violence had broken out.

National Guard troops, such as the 4,000 men who have been called into Memphis, remain under state control until the responsible Governor requests help and the President decides to assume responsibility for restoring order.

David E. McGiffert, Under Secretary of the Army Gen. Harold K. Johnson, the Army Chief of Staff, and the general counsel of the Army, Robert Jordan, went to the Army Operations Center at the Pentagon tonight.

The XVIII Airborne Corps at Fort Bragg, N. C., also opened its emergency operations headquarters tonight. The XVIII Airborne Corps controls the 82d Airborne Division, whose remaining two brigades are the only elite Army troops capable of swift movement to a riot-torn city. The division headquarters was alerted by the corps tonight, but none of the troop units have yet been placed on the alert.

The shock of Dr. King's death, which hit this capital with numbing suddenness, was reflected in the President's face as he spoke to the nation.

In his message, delivered shortly after 9 P.M. Eastern standard time from a doorway of the west wing of the White House, the President said:

"America is shocked and saddened by the brutal slaying tonight of Dr. Martin Luther King. I ask every citizen to reject the blind violence that has struck Dr. King, who lived by nonviolence."

Mr. Johnson said he and Mrs. Johnson had conveyed their sympathy to Mrs. King. "I know," he added, "that every American of good will joins me in mourning the death of this outstanding leader in praying for peace and understanding throughout this land."

The President said that nothing could be achieved by lawlessness and divisiveness among Americans. Only by working together, he asserted, can America move toward full equality and fulfillment for everyone.

"I hope," Mr. Johnson declared solemnly, "that all Americans tonight will search their hearts as they ponder this most tragic incident."

The President and Dr. King developed a close working relationship during Mr. Johhson's first two years in the White House, but it began to cool when the Negro leader became critical of the Administration's Vietnam policies as a costly diversion of resources from pressing domestic needs.

They cooperated in Mr. Johnson's 1964 campaign against Barry Goldwater and, in the development of Great Society programs, including civil rights and voting rights measures. As far as is known, they had no contact in the last year.

The Vice President announced Dr. King's death to the 2,500 persons attending the Congressional dinner. Mr. Humphrey, who was seated at the head table on a raised platform, rose, and in a solemn, heavy voice said:

"This is a very unusual and special and very difficult time. A great tragedy has taken place in America tonight. One of our renowned and active leaders in the cause of civil rights has been stricken down by an assassin's bullet. Martin Luther King has been shot and is dead."

The Vice President then read a prepared statement. "The criminal act that took his life brings shame to our country," he said. "The apostle of nonviolence has been the victim of violence. The cause for which he marched and worked, I am sure, will find new strength."

Mr. Humphrey added: "An America of full freedom, full and equal opportunity, is the living memorial he deserves, and it shall be his living memorial."

Widespread Disorders; Racial Clashes in Several Cities

BY THE NEW YORK TIMES | APRIL 5, 1968

DISORDERS BROKE OUT in scattered parts of the nation last night after the slaying of the Rev. Dr. Martin Luther King Jr. The National Guard was called out or alerted in several cities.

In Washington, scattered but persistent looting and vandalism erupted, led for a time by Stokely Carmichael, former head of the Student Nonviolent Coordinating Committee. All available policemen were being called to duty.

About 4,000 Tennessee National Guardsmen were ordered to duty in Nashville because of disorders.

In North Carolina, Gov. Dan K. Moore alerted the Guard in Greensboro at the request of Mayor Carson Bain. State Highway patrolmen were dispatched to Raleigh.

There were riotous outbursts and brief clashes with the police in Winston-Salem, New Bern, Durham and Charlotte, N. C., and in Jackson, Miss., Boston, Hartford, New York City and Memphis, when Dr. King was killed.

Martin Luther King Jr.: Leader of Millions in Nonviolent Drive for Racial Justice

OBITUARY | BY MURRAY SCHUMACH | APRIL 5, 1968

TO MANY MILLIONS of American Negroes, the Rev. Dr. Martin Luther King Jr. was the prophet of their crusade for racial equality. He was their voice of anguish, their eloquence in humiliation, their battle cry for human dignity. He forged for them the weapons of nonviolence that withstood and blunted the ferocity of Segregation.

And to many millions of American whites, he was one of a group of Negroes who preserved the bridge of communication between races when racial warfare threatened the United States in the nineteen-sixties, as Negroes sought the full emancipation pledged to them a century before by Abraham Lincoln.

To the world Dr. King had the stature that accrued to a winner of the Nobel Peace Prize; a man with access to the White House and the Vatican; a veritable hero in the African states that were just emerging from colonialism.

BETWEEN EXTREMES

In his dedication to nonviolence, Dr. King was caught between white and Negro extremists as racial tensions erupted into arson, gunfire and looting in many of the nation's cities during the summer of 1967.

Militant Negroes, with the cry of, "burn, baby burn," argued that only by violence and segregation could the Negro attain self-respect, dignity and real equality in the United States.

Floyd B. McKissick, then director of the Congress of Racial Equality, declared in August of that year that it was a "foolish assumption to try to sell nonviolence to the ghettos."

And white extremists, not bothering to make distinctions between degrees of Negro militancy, looked upon Dr. King as one of their chief enemies.

At times in recent months, efforts by Dr. King to utilize nonviolent methods exploded into violence.

VIOLENCE IN MEMPHIS

Last week, when he led a protest march through downtown Memphis, Tenn., in support of the city's striking sanitation workers, a group of Negro youths suddenly began breaking store windows and looting, and one Negro was shot to death.

Two days later, however, Dr. King said he would stage another demonstration and attributed the violence to his own "miscalculation."

At the time he was assassinated in Memphis, Dr. King was involved in one of his greatest plans to dramatize the plight of the poor and stir Congress to help Negroes.

He called this venture the "Poor People's Campaign." It was to be a huge "camp-in" either in Washington or in Chicago during the Democratic National Convention.

In one of his last public pronouncements before the shooting, Dr. King told an audience in a Harlem church on March 26, "We need an alternative to riots and to timid supplication. Nonviolence is our most potent weapon."

His strong beliefs in civil rights and nonviolence made him one of the leading opponents of American participation in the war in Vietnam. To him the war was unjust, diverting vast sums away from programs to alleviate the condition of the Negro poor in this country. He called the conflict "one of history's most cruel and senseless wars." Last January he said:

"We need to make clear in this political year, to Congressmen on both sides of the aisle and to the President of the United States that we will no longer vote for men who continue to see the killing of Vietnamese and Americans as the best way of advancing the goals of freedom and self-determination in Southeast Asia."

OBJECT OF MANY ATTACKS

Inevitably, as a symbol of integration, he became the object of unrelenting attacks and vilification. His home was bombed. He was spat upon and mocked. He was struck and kicked. He was stabbed, almost fatally, by a deranged Negro woman. He was frequently thrown into jail. Threats became so commonplace that his wife could ignore burning crosses on the lawn and ominous phone calls. Through it all he adhered to the creed of passive disobedience that infuriated segregationists.

The adulation that was heaped upon him eventually irritated even some Negroes in the civil rights movement who worked hard, but in relative obscurity. They pointed out — and Dr. King admitted — that he was a poor administrator. Sometimes, with sarcasm, they referred to him, privately, as "De Lawd." They noted that Dr. King's successes were built on the labors of many who had gone before him, the non-coms and privates of the civil rights army who fought without benefit of headlines and television cameras.

The Negro extremists he criticized were contemptuous of Dr. King. They dismissed his passion for nonviolence as another form of servility to white people. They called him an "Uncle Tom," and charged that he was hindering the Negro struggle for equality.

Dr. King's belief in nonviolence was subjected to intense pressure in 1966, when some Negro groups adopted the slogan "black power" in the aftermath of civil rights marches into Mississippi and race riots in Northern cities. He rejected the idea, saying:

"The Negro needs the white man to free him from his fears. The white man needs the Negro to free him from his guilt. A doctrine of black supremacy is as evil as a doctrine of white supremacy."

The doctrine of "black power" threatened to split the Negro civil rights movement and antagonize white liberals who had been supporting Negro causes, and Dr. King suggested "militant nonviolence" as a formula for progress with peace.

At the root of his civil rights convictions was an even more profound faith" in the basic goodness of man and the great potential of

American democracy. These beliefs gave to his speeches a fervor that could not be stilled by criticism.

Scores of millions of Americans — white as well as Negro — who sat before television sets in the summer of 1963 to watch the awesome march of some 200,000 Negroes on Washington were deeply stirred when Dr. King, in the shadow of the Lincoln Memorial, said:

"Even though we face the difficulties of today and tomorrow, I still have a dream. I have a dream that one day this nation will rise up and live out the true meaning of its creed: 'We hold these truths to be self-evident, that all men are created equal.' "

And all over the world, men were moved as they read his words of Dec. 10, 1964, when he became the third member of his race to receive the Nobel Peace Prize.

INSISTENT ON MAN'S DESTINY

"I refuse to accept the idea that man is mere flotsam and jetsam in the river of life which surrounds him," he said. "I refuse to accept the view that mankind is so tragically bound to the starless midnight of racism and war that the bright daybreak of peace and brotherhood can never become a reality.

"I refuse to accept the cynical notion that nation after nation must spiral down a militaristic stairway into the hell of thermonuclear destruction. I believe that unarmed truth and unconditional love will have the final word in reality. This is why right, temporarily defeated, is stronger than evil triumphant."

For the poor and unlettered of his own race, Dr. King spoke differently. There he embraced the rhythm and passion of the revivalist and evangelist. Some observers of Dr. King's technique said that others in the movement were more effective in this respect. But Dr. King had the touch, as he illustrated in a church in Albany, Ga., in 1962:

"So listen to me, children: Put on your marching shoes; don'cha get weary; though the path ahead may be dark and dreary; we're walking for freedom, children."

Or there was the meeting in Gadsden, Ala., late in 1963, when he displayed another side of his ability before an audience of poor Negroes. It went as follows:

King: I hear they are beating you.

Audience: Yes, yes.

King: I hear they are cursing you.

Audience: Yes, yes.

King: I hear they are going into your homes and doing nasty things and beating you.

Audience: Yes, yes.

King: Some of you have knives, and I ask you to put them up. Some of you have arms, and I ask you to put them up. Get the weapon of nonviolence, the breastplate of righteousness, the armor of truth, and just keep marching.

It was said that so devoted was his vast following that even among illiterates he could, by calm discussion of Platonic dogma, evoke deep cries of "Amen."

Dr. King also had a way of reducing complex issues to terms that anyone could understand. Thus, in the summer of 1965, when there was widespread discontent among Negroes about their struggle for equality of employment, he declared:

"What good does it do to be able to eat at a lunch counter if you can't buy a hamburger."

The enormous impact of Dr. King's words was one of the reasons he was in the President's Room in the Capitol on Aug. 6, 1965, when President Johnson signed the Voting Rights Act that struck down literacy tests, provided Federal registrars to assure the ballot to unregistered Negroes and marked the growth of the Negro as a political force in the South.

BACKED BY ORGANIZATION

Dr. King's effectiveness was enhanced and given continuity by the fact that he had an organization behind him. Formed in 1960, with headquarters in Atlanta, it was called the Southern Christian Leadership Conference, familiarly known as SLICK. Allied with it was another organization formed under Dr. King's sponsorship, the Student Nonviolent Coordinating Committee, often referred to as SNICK.

These two organizations reached the country, though their basic strength was in the South. They brought together Negro clergymen, businessmen, professional men and students. They raised the money and planned the sit-ins, the campaigns for Negro vote registration, the demonstrations by which Negroes hacked away at segregationist resistance, lowering the barriers against Negroes in the political, economic and social life of the nation.

This minister, who became the most famous spokesman for Negro rights since Booker T. Washington, was not particularly impressive in appearance. About 5 feet 8 inches tall, he had an oval face with almond-shaped eyes that looked almost dreamy when he was off the platform. His neck and shoulders were heavily muscled, but his hands were almost delicate.

SPEAKER OF FEW GESTURES

There was little of the rabblerouser in his oratory. He was not prone to extravagant gestures or loud peroration. His baritone voice, though vibrant, was not that of a spellbinder. Occasionally, after a particularly telling sentence, he would tilt his head a bit and fall silent as though waiting for the echoes of his thought to spread through the hall, church or street.

In private gatherings, Dr. King lacked the laughing gregariousness that often makes for popularity. Some thought he was without a sense of humor. He was not a gifted raconteur. He did not have the flamboyance of a Representative Adam Clayton Powell Jr. or the cool strategic brilliance of Roy Wilkins, head of the National Association for the Advancement of Colored People.

What Dr. King did have was an instinct for the right moment to make his moves. Some critics looked upon this as pure opportunism.

Nevertheless, it was this sense of timing that raised him in 1955, from a newly arrived minister in Montgomery, Ala., with his first church, to a figure of national prominence.

BUS BOYCOTT IN PROGRESS

Negroes in that city had begun a boycott of buses to win the right to sit where they pleased instead of being forced to move to the rear of buses, in Southern tradition or to surrender seats to white people when a bus was crowded.

The 381-day boycott by Negroes was already under way when the young pastor was placed in charge of the campaign. It has been said that one of the reasons he got the job was because he was so new in the area he had not antagonized any of the Negro factions. Even while the boycott was under way, a board of directors handled the bulk of administrative work.

However, it was Dr. King who dramatized the boycott with his decision to make it the testing ground, before the eyes of the nation, of his belief in the civil disobedience teachings of Thoreau and Gandhi. When he was arrested during the Montgomery boycott, he said:

"If we are arrested every day, if we are exploited every day, if we are trampled over every day, don't ever let anyone pull you so low as to hate them. We must use the weapon of love. We must have compassion and understanding for those who hate us. We must realize so many people are taught to hate us that they are not totally responsible for their hate. But we stand in life at midnight; we are always on the threshold of a new dawn."

HOME BOMBED IN ABSENCE

Even more dramatic, in some ways, was his reaction to the bombing of his home during the boycott. He was away at the time and rushed back fearful for his wife and children. They were not injured. But when he reached the modest house, more than a thousand Negroes had already gathered and were in an ugly mood, seeking revenge against the white people. The police were jittery. Quickly, Dr. King pacified the crowd and there was no trouble.

Dr. King was even more impressive during the "big push" in Birmingham, which began in April 1963. With the minister in the limelight, Negroes there began a campaign of sit-ins at lunch counters, picketing and protest marches. Hundreds of children, used in the campaign, were jailed.

The entire world was stirred when the police turned dogs on the demonstrators. Dr. King was jailed for five days. While he was in prison he issued a 9,000-word letter that created considerable controversy among white people, alienating some sympathizers who thought Dr. King was being too aggressive.

MODERATES CALLED OBSTACLES

In the letter he wrote:

"I have almost reached the regrettable conclusion that the Negro's great stumbling block in the stride toward freedom is not the White Citizens Councilor or the Ku Klux Klanner, but the white moderate who is more devoted to order than to justice; who prefers a negative peace, which is the absence of tension, to a positive peace, which is the presence of justice."

Some critics of Dr. King said that one reason for this letter was to answer Negro intellectuals, such as the writer James Baldwin, who were impatient with Dr. King's belief in brotherhood. Whatever the reasons, the role of Dr. King in Birmingham added to his stature and showed that his enormous following was deeply devoted to him.

He demonstrated this in a threatening situation in Albany, Ga., after four Negro girls were killed in the bombing of a church. Dr. King said at the funeral:

"In spite of the darkness of this hour, we must not despair. We must not lose faith in our white brothers."

As Dr. King's words grew more potent and he was invited to the White House by Presidents Kennedy and Johnson, some critics —

Negroes as well as white — noted that sometimes, despite all the publicity he attracted, he left campaigns unfinished or else failed to attain his goals.

Dr. King was aware of this. But he pointed out, in 1964, in St. Augustine, Fla., one of the toughest civil rights battlegrounds, that there were important intangibles.

"Even if we do not get all we should," he said, "movements such as this tend more and more to give a Negro the sense of self-respect that he needs. It tends to generate courage in Negroes outside the movement. It brings intangible results outside the community where it is carried out. There is a hardening of attitudes in situations like this. But other cities see and say: 'We don't want to be another Albany or Birmingham,' and they make changes. Some communities, like this one, had to bear the cross."

It was in this city that Negroes marched into the fists of the mob singing: "We love everybody."

CONSCIOUS OF LEADING ROLE

There was no false modesty in Dr. King's self-appraisal of his role in the civil rights movement.

"History," he said, "has thrust me into this position. It would be both immoral and a sign of ingratitude if I did not face my moral responsibility to do what I can in this struggle."

Another time he compared himself to Socrates as one of "the creative gadflies of society."

At times he addressed himself deliberately to the white people of the nation. Once, he said:

"We will match your capacity to inflict suffering with our capacity to endure suffering. We will meet your physical force with soul force. We will not hate you, but we cannot in all good conscience obey your unjust laws .... We will soon wear you down by our capacity to suffer. And in winning our freedom we will so appeal to your heart and conscience that we will win you in the process."

The enormous influence of Dr. King's voice in the turbulent racial conflict reached into New York in 1964. In the summer of that year racial rioting exploded in New York and in other Northern cities with large Negro populations. There was widespread fear that the disorders, particularly in Harlem, might set off unprecedented racial violence.

At this point Dr. King became one of the major intermediaries in restoring order. He conferred with Mayor Robert F. Wagner and with Negro leaders. A statement was issued, of which he was one of the signers, calling for "a broad curtailment if not total moratorium on mass demonstrations until after Presidential elections."

The following year, Dr. King was once more in the headlines and on television — this time leading a drive for Negro voter registration in Selma, Ala. Negroes were arrested by the hundreds. Dr. King was punched and kicked by a white man when, during this period of protest, he became the first Negro to register at a century-old hotel in Selma.

Martin Luther King Jr. was born Jan. 15, 1929, in Atlanta on Auburn Avenue. As a child his name was Michael Luther King and so was his father's. His father changed both their names legally to Martin Luther King in honor of the Protestant reformer.

Auburn Avenue is one of the nation's most widely known Negro sections. Many successful Negro business or professional men have lived there. The Rev. Martin Luther King Sr. was pastor of the Ebenezer Baptist Church at Jackson Street and Auburn Avenue.

Young Martin went to Atlanta's Morehouse College, a Negro institution whose students acquired what was sometimes called the "Morehouse swank." The president of Morehouse, Dr. B. E. Mays, took a special interest in Martin, who had decided, in his junior year, to be a clergyman.

He was ordained a minister in his father's church in 1947. It was in this church he was to say, some years later:

"America, you've strayed away. You've trampled over 19 million of your brethren. All men are created equal. Not some men. Not white men. All men. America, rise up and come home."

Before Dr. King had his own church he pursued his studies in the integrated Crozier Theological Seminary, in Chester, Pa. He was one of six Negroes in a student body of about a hundred. He became the first Negro class president. He was named the outstanding student and won a fellowship to study for a doctorate at the school of his choice. The young man enrolled at Boston College in 1951.

For his doctoral thesis he sought to resolve the differences between the Harvard theologian Paul Tillich and the neonaturalist philosopher Henry Nelson Wieman. During this period he took courses at Harvard as well.

While he was working on his doctorate he met Coretta Scott, a graduate of Antioch College, who was doing graduate work in music. He married the singer in 1953. They had four children, Yolanda, Martin Luther King 3d, Dexter Scott and Bernice.

In 1954, Dr. King became pastor of the Dexter Avenue Baptist Church in Montgomery, Ala. At that time few of Montgomery's white residents saw any reason for a major dispute with the city's 50,000 Negroes. They did not seem to realize how deeply the Negroes resented segregated seating on buses, for instance.

REVOLT BEGUN BY WOMAN

On Dec. 1, 1955, they learned, almost by accident. Mrs. Rosa Parks, a Negro seamstress, refused to comply with a bus driver's order to give up her seat to a white passenger. She was tired, she said. Her feet hurt from a day of shopping.

Mrs. Parks had been a local secretary for the National Association for the Advancement of Colored people. She was arrested, convicted of refusing to obey the bus conductor and fined $10 and costs, a total of $14. Almost as spontaneous as Mrs. Parks's act was the rallying of many Negro leaders in the city to help her.

From a protest begun over a Negro woman's tired feet Dr. King began his public career.

In 1959 Dr. King and his family moved back to Atlanta, where he became a co-pastor, with his father, of the Ebenezer Baptist Church.

As his fame increased, public interest in his beliefs led him to write books. It was while he was autographing one of these books, "Stride Toward Freedom," in a Harlem department store that he was stabbed by a Negro woman.

It was in these books that he summarized, in detail, his beliefs as well as his career. Thus, in "Why We Can't Wait," he wrote:

"The Negro knows he is right. He has not organized for conquest or to gain spoils or to enslave those who have injured him. His goal is not to capture that which belongs to someone else. He merely wants, and will have, what is honorably his."

The possibility that he might someday be assassinated was considered by Dr. King on June 5, 1964, when he reported, in St. Augustine, Fla., that his life had been threatened. He said:

"Well, if physical death is the price that I must pay to free my white brothers and sisters from a permanent death of the spirit, then nothing can be more redemptive."

Plea, by Mrs. King: 'Fulfill His Dream'

BY WALTER RUGABER | APRIL 7, 1968

ATLANTA, APRIL 6 — Mrs. Martin Luther King Jr. urged today that her slain husband's followers "join us in fulfilling his dream" of "a creative rather than a destructive way" out of the nation's racial problems.

Her plea, delivered in the sanctuary of the Ebenezer Baptist Church, which Dr. King had served as co-pastor, came as the violence and death sparked by her husband's assassination in Memphis Thursday raged through a number of the nation's major cities.

"He gave his life for the poor of the world — the garbage workers of Memphis and the peasants of Vietnam," Mrs. King said. Dr. King had gone to Memphis to organize a march in support of the city's striking sanitation employees.

"Nothing hurt him more than that man could attempt no way to solve problems except through violence," the widow continued. "He gave his life in search of a more excellent way, a more effective way, a creative rather than a destructive way."

Mrs. King, wearing a black dress and speaking in a clear and steady voice, said at a news conference that "we intend to go on in search of that way, and I hope that you who loved and admired him would join us in fulfilling his dream."

Services for Dr. King are scheduled to begin at 10:30 A.M. Tuesday with brief worship at the Ebenezer Church, where Dr. King had served with his father, the Rev. Dr. Martin Luther King Sr.

Then the mourners are to march through the city to Morehouse College, the predominantly Negro institution that Dr. King attended as an undergraduate. A longer service, set for 1 P.M., will be outdoors in the quadrangle there.

The church has a limited seating capacity. However, the Rev. Ralph D. Abernathy said the quadrangle, together with adjoining areas of the campus that will be connected by a public address system, could accommodate as many as 100,000 persons.

Mr. Abernathy, who succeeded Dr. King as president of the Southern Christian Leadership Conference, appeared before the newsmen with Mrs. King.

The slain leader's wife asked that "friends, supporters, and well-wishers," instead of sending flowers, send funds for the continuation of Dr. King's work to the leadership conference at 1334 Auburn Avenue, N.E., Atlanta, Ga., 30303.

HUNDREDS FILE PAST

Today, hundreds of mourners gathered to file past Dr. King's body, scheduled to lie in state until 4 P.M. Monday at Sister's Chapel on the campus of Spelman College, a girl's school near Morehouse.

The throngs began filing past the open coffin shortly after 6:30 P.M. They were delayed for about an hour while Mrs. King, accompanied by several members of the family and friends, entered the chapel privately.

With the widow were Dr. King's brother, the Rev. A. D. Williams King; his sister, Mrs. Christine Farris; his mother, Mrs. Martin Luther King Sr.; his secretary, Miss Dora McDonald, and Harry Belafonte, the singer.

The coffin in which the body returned from Memphis yesterday has been exchanged for one of mahogany. The new coffin rested on a portable stand, with about two dozen floral arrangements nearby. Dr. King was dressed in a black suit and a white shirt.

EXECUTIVES AND DOMESTICS

The mourners, who ranged from business men dressed in conservative suits to domestic workers wearing aprons, often displayed emotion. One woman fainted, and a second nearly did so as she passed the coffin.

Some snapped pictures, but the crowd was orderly and obeyed when ushers urged them to move on. Several of Dr. King's aides stood by in the chapel, where an organist played solemn music.

There was a scattering of whites among those waiting. No trouble was reported. On Monday, the body will be brought to the church to lie in state there until the funeral begins at 10:30 A.M.

APPEARS AT CHURCH

Mrs. King had been invited to make her statement at a local television studio to permit a live national broadcast. But she refused to appear except at the Ebenezer Baptist Church. Technical difficulties prevented live telecasting there.

An informed source said it was first thought that Dr. King's father might make the statement, and a stronger and more direct plea for nonviolence was drafted for him last night before Mrs. King decided to make her remarks.

Mrs. King did not refer directly to racial violence in the nation during her 11-minute appearance before newspaper reporters and television cameramen this afternoon. She left the church immediately after making the statement.

Mrs. King sat at a narrow wooden table before the pulpit. Behind her, high on a wall of the church, was a stained glass window depicting a praying Christ. Cameras clicked constantly as she spoke.

Blinking into the bright lights, the widow said she would have preferred to be alone with her children. She said that "the response from so many friends around the world has been very comforting to us.

"He knew that at any moment his physical life could be cut short," Mrs. King said, "and we faced this squarely and honestly. My husband faced the possibility of death without bitterness or hatred."

She continued: "He knew that this was a sick society, totally infested with racism and violence that questioned his integrity, maligned his motives, and distorted his views, and he struggled with every ounce of his energy to save that society from itself.

"He never hated, he never despaired of well-doing, and he encouraged us to do likewise. I am surprised and pleased at the success of his teaching, for our children say calmly, 'Daddy is not dead. He may be physically dead, but his spirit will never die.' "

Leaders at Rites; High and Lowly Join in Last Tribute to Rights Champion

BY HOMER BIGART | APRIL 10, 1968

ATLANTA, APRIL 9 — The coffin of the Rev. Dr. Martin Luther King Jr. was carried through the streets of Atlanta today on a crude farm wagon pulled by two Georgia mules. It was followed by tens of thousands of mourners, black and white, the lowly and the powerful, mingling in silent tribute to the slain Negro civil rights leader.

It was one of the strangest corteges ever seen in the land.

The body of Dr. King, the advocate of racial progress through nonviolence, who was shot by a sniper last Thursday in Memphis, lay in a gleaming African mahogany coffin that rested on the rough planks of the faded green cart. The wagon and the mules were symbols of Dr. King's identification with the poor.

IN 80-DEGREE HEAT

Behind the wagon marched some of the nation's highest figures in finance, politics, religion and government. In sultry 80-degree heat Governor Rockefeller of New York and Senator Robert F. Kennedy made the three-and-one-half-mile walk from Ebenezer Baptist Church, where a funeral service was held, across the city to an open air general service at Morehouse College.

The service at the church began at 10:43 AM, 13 minutes after the scheduled start. By the time the march from the church to the college and the 90-minute memorial service there were over, it was 5:30 P.M. before Dr. King was buried in South View Cemetery.

The Atlanta police declined to estimate the size of the crowd, but unofficial estimates put the number of marchers at about 50,000, with perhaps 100,000 more viewing the procession and the service on the campus.

DON HOGAN CHARLES/THE NEW YORK TIMES

At the funeral procession for the Rev. Dr. Martin Luther King Jr., Coretta King walked with the Rev. A. D. King, left, the Rev. Ralph D. Abernathy, and her children, from the left, Yolanda, Beatrice, Dexter and Martin Luther 3rd.

MANY IN THRONG FAINT

Observers estimated the proportion of whites in the procession and at the two services at about 10 per cent. Dozens of mourners fainted from the heat and the pressing of the crowds.

All of the avowed candidates for Presidential nomination attended the service in Ebenezer Church, where Dr. King was copastor with his father.

Besides Senator Kennedy of New York, the mourners included his rival for the Democratic nomination, Senator Eugene J. McCarthy of Minnesota. Former Vice President Richard M. Nixon, the only announced major candidate for the Republican nomination, was there.

Representing the White House was Vice President Humphrey, who is expected to announce for the Democratic nomination soon.

Although the visiting politicians were received courteously by the largely middle-class Negro crowd and Senator Kennedy was cheered, cries of "politicking" greeted Mr. Nixon as he entered the church.

Some of the younger militants murmured privately about "crocodile tears" and vote-seeking.

In the throng there were too, a scattering of bishops in ecclesiastical robes, some African envoys, labor potentates and some famous Negro names in the theater, the cinema and sports.

From Washington came 50 members of the House of Representatives and 30 Senators. A regiment of Mayors appeared, some of them from cities recently torn by riots.

But the figure that evoked the sharpest pang of sentiment was Mrs. John F. Kennedy, widowed — like Coretta King — by an assassin.

PULLED INTO CHURCH

Recognized by surging crowds as she was led toward the church, Mrs. Kennedy was suddenly caught up in such a pressure of people that she had to be pulled and pushed through the narrow door. For a moment her face appeared strained and frightened.

Soon after Mrs. Kennedy disappeared through the door, there was another commotion. Stokely Carmichael, the black power apostle, appeared, wearing a light blue turtleneck sweater under a dark coat and accompanied by six bodyguards.

The church was already jammed — Governor Rockefeller, Mayor Lindsay of New York and Gov. George Romney of Michigan had yielded their seats to women and were standing in the aisle. Carmichael had been invited — there was a seat for him — but the doormen were dubious about the bodyguards.

So there was a milling confrontation at the entrance. Some of Carmichael's followers, thinking he himself was being kept out, shouted: "You'd better let him in" and "He's a black man." Finally the whole group was allowed to enter.

SERVICE IS DELAYED

At times the clamor for admission was loud enough to disturb the service, which had started late because the principal mourners, including the immediate family, were unable to get into the church.

Dr. King's brother, the Rev. A. D. King, emerged to appeal for order. Stepping onto the back of a black hearse that was to be used to carry flowers, he pleaded:

"At this hour our hearts are very heavy. Please let the family through. You would want Dr. King's wife, children, mother and father to have an opportunity of seeing this service. Please don't make Mrs. King have to fight her way in.

No one budged. Dr. King's brother said, "If we can't receive your cooperation, we have but one choice — to remove the body and bury it privately."

Then there was less tumult and jostling. Inside the church. Governors Rockefeller and Romney and Mayor Lindsay were led to seats at the center of the church. Mrs. Kennedy sat next to Senator Edward M. Kennedy of Massachusetts, near the front. Vice President Humphrey, who entered through a side door just before the service started, walked up close to the coffin and greeted Dr. King's parents in the front row.

On the closed coffin, beneath the central pulpit, was a large cross of white chrysanthemums and white lilies. The coffin was flanked by banks of roses, chrysanthemums and lilies.

There was only one touch of incongruity. The nose of a television camera protruded through red velvet curtains, that hung behind the pulpit, under an electric cross and a round stained-glass window with the figure of Jesus kneeling in prayer.

BISHOPS AT FUNERAL

Seated among the New York delegation were the Right Rev. Horace W. B. Donegan, Episcopal Bishop of New York; the Most Rev. Terence J. Cooke, the new Roman Catholic Archbishop of New York, whose bright purple episcopal robes made him conspicuous among the mourners; Archbishop Iakovos, Greek Orthodox primate of North and South America, and Rabbi Henry Siegman, executive vice president of the Synagogue Council of America.

At the request of Mrs. King the church service included a taped excerpt from the last sermon Dr. King preached at the church, on Feb. 4.

The congregation was visibly moved, and some wept openly, as the voice of Dr. King said, "If any of you are around when I have to meet my day, I don't want a long funeral. And if you get somebody to deliver the eulogy, tell him not to talk too long .... Tell him not to mention that I have a Nobel Peace Prize — that isn't important.

"Tell him not to mention that I have 300 or 400 other awards — that's not important.

"Tell him not to mention where I went to school.

"I'd like somebody to mention that day that Martin Luther King Jr. tried to give his life serving others.

"I'd like for somebody to say that day that Martin Luther King Jr. tried to love somebody ....

"I want you to be able to I say that day that I did try to feed the hungry. I want you to be able to say that day that I did try in my life to clothe the naked. I want you to say on that day that I did try in my life to visit those who were in prison. And I want you to say that I tried to love and serve humanity."

'ONE OF THE DARKEST HOURS'

The Rev. Ralph D. Abernathy, who succeeds Dr. King as president of the Southern Christian Leadership Conference, opened the church service by calling Dr. King's murder "one of the darkest hours of mankind."

A brief tribute to Dr. King was delivered by Dr. L. Harold DeWolfe, dean of Wesley Theological Seminary, Washington, who had taught Dr. King at Boston University. Dr. DeWolfe, the only white participant in the service, said that "Dr. King sought to relieve the slavery of the oppressors as well as that of the oppressed."

"It is now for us, all the millions of the living who care, to take up his torch of love," he said. "It is for us to finish his work, to end the awful destruction in Vietnam, to root out every trace of race prejudice from our lives, to bring the massive powers of this nation to aid the oppressed and to heal the hate-scarred world."

The service was an hour longer than expected, and it was past noon when the coffin was carried out and placed on the cart. Many of the dignitaries did not make the march. Others dropped out along the way.

The procession moved down Auburn Street, past a clutter of closed taverns and honky-tonks and into the downtown business district. Here the sidewalk crowds were predominantly white.

Most of the men doffed their hats as the mule wagon passed. A few who did not do so obeyed quickly when marchers politely asked them to.

The line of march led past the domed State Capitol, where the segregationist Governor, Lester G. Maddox, was sitting in his office, under heavy guard.

Governor Maddox's decision not to participate in the funeral was hailed by Charles Morgan Jr., one of the three white directors of the Southern Christian Leadership Conference, as "an honest act at a time when very few honest acts are performed."

"Of course," Mr. Morgan added, "the Governor's attendance would have been a desecration."

Without bands, the procession seemed strangely silent as it toiled past City Hall, draped in mourning. But as the marchers moved over the long Hunter Street viaduct into the largely Negro West Side, they occasionally broke into the songs that Dr. King loved, "We Shall Overcome" and "This Little Light of Mine."

It was nearly 3 P.M. by the time the memorial service began on the campus of Morehouse College, where Dr. King had been an undergraduate. Again the crush of crowds around Dr. King's family became so great that the service was interrupted for nearly 15 minutes while clergymen pleaded with the people to stand back. Many fainted.

'A LOVE AND CONCERN FOR ALL'

In the eulogy at Morehouse, Dr. Benjamin H. Mays, president emeritus of Morehouse, said:

"I make bold to assert that it took more courage for King to practice nonviolence than it took his assassin to fire the fatal shot.

"The assassin is a coward: he committed his foul act and fled. When Martin Luther disobeyed an unjust law, he accepted the consequences of his actions. He never ran away and he never begged for mercy."

Dr. Mays said that although Dr. King was "deeply committed to a program of freedom for Negroes, he had a love and concern for all kinds of people."

"He drew no distinction between the high and low; none between the rich and poor," he said. "He believed especially that he was sent to champion the cause of the man farthest down. He would probably say that, if death had to come, I'm sure there was no greater cause to die for than fighting to get a just wage for garbage collectors.

"He was supra-race, supra-nation, supra-denomination, supra-class and supra-culture. He belonged to the world and to mankind. Now he belongs to posterity."

Dr. King was shot while in Memphis aiding the cause of the city's sanitation men, who are seeking city recognition of their union.

By the time the march reached the campus, the ranks of dignitaries were badly depleted. The few that endured looked wilted.

SERVICE CUT SHORT

On the campus so many mourners became ill that the service there was abbreviated. Scheduled tributes by the Mayor of Atlanta, Ivan Allen Jr., a close friend of Dr. King, by Mrs. Rosa Parks, whose refusal to take a back seat in a bus in Montgomery, Ala., started Dr. King's civil rights career, and by the Most Rev. James Wright, Roman Catholic Bishop of Pittsburgh, were not given.

Protocol also received short shrift. Mr. Abernathy called upon Robert Kennedy to come to the platform, seeming to ignore Governor Rockefeller and other dignitaries scattered about the campus. Prompted by persons in the crowd, Mr. Abernathy invited Governor Rockefeller and "all other Governors and Senators" to the platform.

Senator Jacob K. Javits of New York was one of the first to oblige. Mr. Abernathy also called for Mr. Nixon and Vice President Humphrey, but they had departed after the church service.

South View Cemetery, where Dr. King was buried, was abloom with dogwood and the fresh green boughs of April.

Crowds of Negroes and whites had lined the four-mile route from the campus to the cemetery. The little hillside graveyard was founded in 1866, right after the Civil War, by six Negroes who were tired of taking their dead to the back gates of the municipal cemeteries.

Dr. King's coffin was taken from the college to the cemetery in a hearse.

The interment rites were brief. Mr. Abernathy intoned:

"The cemetery is too small for his spirit but we submit his body to the ground. The grave is too narrow for his soul, but we commit his body to the ground. No coffin, no crypt, no stone can hold his greatness. But we submit his body to the ground."

Dr. King was buried beside his grandparents. An epitaph on the tombstone, derived from a Negro spiritual, reads:

> *"Free at last; free at last; thank God Almighty I'm free at last."*

The body of Dr. King may remain at South View for only about six months. There is talk of removing it to a memorial shrine on the Morehouse campus.

Tongue-Tied Justice

OPINION | BY THE NEW YORK TIMES | MARCH 11, 1969

THE ABORTED TRIAL of James Earl Ray for the assassination of Dr. Martin Luther King Jr. is a shocking breach of faith with the American people, black and white, and of people the world over still numbed and puzzled by the gunfire that struck down this international leader.

Ray is entitled by all legal means to avail himself of the defenses open to him under the law. But by no means, legal or pragmatic, should the doors of the courtroom and the jail be slammed shut on the facts, the motives and the doubts of this horrible murder.

And yet that is just what has occurred with stunning suddenness in a Memphis courthouse. By pleading guilty, Ray has been sentenced to 99 years in prison. The jury had to go along with this prearranged deal between the prosecution and the admitted killer's attorney. Circuit Judge W. Preston Battle went along with it too, treating the whole matter as if it were a routine murder case.

Nothing but outrage and suspicion can follow the handling of this long-delayed and instantly snuffed-out trial. Percy Foreman, the defense lawyer, tells the public that it took him months "to prove to myself" that Ray was not part of a murder conspiracy. Ray himself acquiesces in the bargain made on the guilty plea — then says publicly that he refuses to go along with the statement that there was no conspiracy.

Why should this assassination case be tried by statements instead of formal legal procedures, subject to examination and cross-examination, the presentation of all the evidence by the prosecution, the appearance of the accused in open court? What in either sense or jurisprudence does it mean that the defense attorney convinced himself? In the ghetto and in the world outside the ghetto, the question still cries for answer: Was there a conspiracy to kill Dr. King and who was in it?

The state's case has been read to the jury. But that is hardly enough in a case of this magnitude. This was not a street crime but, on the surface, a racist or quasi-political assassination. It is not enough to say that the state accepted the guilty plea and agreed to end the case because the death penalty has not been used since 1961 in Tennessee.

No one was demanding blood; everyone is demanding facts. Are we going to get the facts from Ray's lawyers, past or present, one of whom is trying to peddle the story to magazines? Are we going to get the facts from William Bradford Huie, the author who has "bought" the "rights" to Ray's story? What a mockery of justice for the facts to emerge in marketed justice!

Unless proceedings are convened in court — Federal, if not state — we shall never know the adjudicated truth. There should be no Warren Commissions necessary — a month or a year from now — to still our doubts and do what a Tennessee court has failed to do.

How Dr. King Lived Is Why He Died

BY JESSE JACKSON | APRIL 4, 2018

AS THE NATION prepares to commemorate the 50th anniversary of the assassination of the Rev. Dr. Martin Luther King Jr., we cannot merely dwell on how Dr. King died, but also on how he lived.

He mobilized mass action to win a public accommodations bill and the right to vote. He led the Montgomery bus boycott and navigated police terror in Birmingham. He got us over the bloodstained bridge in Selma and survived the rocks and bottles and hatred in Chicago. He globalized our struggle to end the war in Vietnam.

How he lived is why he died.

As he sought to move beyond desegregation and the right to vote and to focus on economic justice, antimilitarism and human rights, the system pushed back hard. In the last months of his life, he was attacked by the government, the press, former allies and the military industrial complex. Even black Democrats turned their backs on him when he challenged the party's support for the war in Vietnam.

A growing number of Americans had a negative view of Dr. King in the final years of his life, according to public opinion polls. A man of peace, he died violently. A man of love, he died hated by many.

America loathes marchers but loves martyrs. The bullet in Memphis made Dr. King a martyr for the ages.

We owe it to Dr. King — and to our children and grandchildren — to commemorate the man in full: a radical, ecumenical, antiwar, pro-immigrant and scholarly champion of the poor who spent much more time marching and going to jail for liberation and justice than he ever spent dreaming about it.

This is a painful time of the year for me because it is when I am asked to remember the most traumatic night in my life.

We had come to Memphis in 1968 to support striking sanitation workers in their fight for better wages and safer working conditions. On the evening of April 4, Dr. King was going to take a group of us, including the Rev. Ralph Abernathy, Andy Young, Hosea Williams and Bernard Lee, to dinner at the home of the Rev. Billy Kyles, not far from where we were staying, the Lorraine Motel.

As we prepared to go, Dr. King cheerfully admonished me, the youngest of the group, for not being suitably dressed for the evening. I wasn't wearing a tie. "Doc, the only prerequisite for dinner," I joked back, "is an appetite, not a tie."

We laughed. Dr. King loved to laugh.

After dinner we were going to attend a rally for the sanitation workers. I had brought the Operation Breadbasket Orchestra from Chicago to play at the rally. Dr. King, always the hottest ticket in any town, was scheduled to speak. He'd be hard pressed, though, to top the speech he gave the night before at the Mason Temple in Memphis, where he pledged that "we, as a people, will get to the promised land."

It was raining cats and dogs, but the Mason Temple, part of the Church of God in Christ, was nearly full. I was sitting behind Dr. King on the pulpit. He spoke with such pathos and passion that I saw grown men wiping away tears in the sanctuary. "I'm not worried about anything," Dr. King told the crowd of about 3,000. "I'm not fearing any man. Mine eyes have seen the glory of the coming of the Lord."

None of us took those words as a premonition. We had heard similar sentiments from him before. Maybe we were in denial. While danger was all around, we never thought the Martin Luther King we knew and loved, admitted to Morehouse College at 15, graduated and ordained at 19, a Ph.D. at 26, awarded the Nobel Peace Prize at 35, would be dead at 39.

On April 4, the fatal shot rang out just after 6 p.m. as we were about to get into the cars to go to dinner. Dr. King was on the balcony of the Lorraine Motel. I was in the parking lot below.

A couple of hours later, Mr. Abernathy, Dr. King's successor, gathered us at the Lorraine. By then much of urban America had already moved from shock and sorrow to rage and flames. We had a choice: Surrender to our own anguish and anger, or honor the slain prince of peace by picking up the baton of nonviolent direct action.

With deep breaths, the baton firmly in our hands, we went to Resurrection City, the tent city erected by Dr. King's Poor People's Campaign in Washington, and continued the work of ending poverty and the war. As the Rev. Joseph Lowery said, we would not let one bullet kill the movement.

Dr. King's spirit has been our moral guidepost for 50 years. That spirit is alive today with the high school students of Parkland, Fla., as they push the country toward sensible gun control. It is alive with the teachers of West Virginia, who are blazing a trail for other workers. It is alive with Black Lives Matter, the Dreamers, Colin Kaepernick and thousands of African-American voters who defied the pundits and sent an Alabama Democrat to the Senate for the first time in a generation. It is alive with the Rev. William Barber as he resurrects Dr. King's last crusade, the Poor People's Campaign.

He bequeathed African-Americans the will to resist and the right to vote. Yet while we were marching and winning, the powers of reaction were regrouping, preparing a counter revolution. Five decades ago, a segregationist governor, George Wallace, peddled hate and division in reaction to the civil rights movement. Today, it is the president himself who is inciting anguish, bigotry and fear.

We are in a battle for the soul of America, and it's not enough to admire Dr. King. To admire him is to reduce him to a mere celebrity. It requires no commitment, no action. Those who value justice and equality must have the will and courage to follow him. They must be ready to sacrifice.

The struggle continues.

THE REV. JESSE JACKSON, A FORMER AIDE TO THE REV. DR. MARTIN LUTHER KING JR., IS THE FOUNDER AND PRESIDENT OF THE RAINBOW PUSH COALITION.

Glossary

assassination The act of murdering someone for political reasons.

black consciousness An awareness of one's identity as a black person, and as a member of a political group or movement.

civil disobedience The refusal of a citizen to obey certain laws, demands, orders or commands of the government.

civil rights Rights that ensure one's ability to participate in the civil and political life of a country without discrimination or oppression.

communist A person who supports the principles of communism, the political model wherein all property is publicly owned and each person is paid according to their abilities and needs.

cortege A procession of people, particularly for a funeral.

demonstrator A participant in a public protest or march.

desegregation The policy of ending separation by race.

disorders States of unrest; sometimes indicates rioting, looting or vandalism.

loot To steal goods from businesses or homes during a protest or riot.

nonviolent resistance The practice of achieving social change through nonviolent practices such as symbolic protests, boycotts, civil disobedience, or economic or political noncooperation.

racial discrimination The unfair treatment of different groups of people based on race.

rout A disorderly group of people causing confusion.

segregation Separation of racial groups in daily life.

Media Literacy Terms

"Media literacy" refers to the ability to access, understand, critically assess and create media. The following terms are important components of media literacy, and they will help you critically engage with the articles in this title.

angle The aspect of a news story on which a journalist focuses and develops.

attribution The method by which a source is identified or by which facts and information are assigned to the person who provided them.

balance Principle of journalism that both perspectives of an argument should be presented in a fair way.

chronological order Method of writing a story presenting the details of the story in the order in which they occurred.

commentary Type of story that is an expression of opinion on recent events by a journalist generally known as a commentator.

credibility The quality of being trustworthy and believable, said of a journalistic source.

critical review Type of story that describes an event or work of art, such as a theater performance, film, concert, book, restaurant, radio or television program, exhibition or musical piece, and offers critical assessment of its quality and reception.

editorial Article of opinion or interpretation.

feature story Article designed to entertain as well as to inform.

headline Type, usually 18 point or larger, used to introduce a story.

human interest story Type of story that focuses on individuals and how events or issues affect their lives, generally offering a sense of relatability to the reader.

impartiality Principle of journalism that a story should not reflect a journalist's bias and should contain balance.

intention The motive or reason behind something, such as the publication of a news story.

interview story Type of story in which the facts are gathered primarily by interviewing another person or persons.

motive The reason behind something, such as the publication of a news story or a source's perspective on an issue.

news story An article or style of expository writing that reports news, generally in a straightforward fashion and without editorial comment.

op-ed An opinion piece that reflects a prominent individual's opinion on a topic of interest.

paraphrase The summary of an individual's words, with attribution, rather than a direct quotation of their exact words.

quotation The use of an individual's exact words indicated by the use of quotation marks and proper attribution.

reliability The quality of being dependable and accurate, said of a journalistic source.

rhetorical device Technique in writing intending to persuade the reader or communicate a message from a certain perspective.

source The origin of the information reported in journalism.

style A distinctive use of language in writing or speech; also a news or publishing organization's rules for consistent use of language with regards to spelling, punctuation, typography and capitalization, usually regimented by a house style guide.

tone A manner of expression in writing or speech.

Media Literacy Questions

1. What is the intention of the article "Negroes Pledge to Keep Boycott" (on page 9)? How effectively does Wayne Phillips achieve his purpose?

2. "Battle Against Tradition; Martin Luther King Jr." (on page 12) is an example of a feature story. What is the purpose of a feature story? Does this article achieve that purpose?

3. Does Claude Sitton demonstrate the journalistic principle of impartiality in his article "Dr. King, Symbol Of the Segregation Struggle" (on page 49)? If so, how? If not, how could he have made his article more impartial?

4. "Dr. King to Weigh Civil Disobedience If War Intensifies" (on page 96) is an example of an interview. What are the benefits of providing readers with direct quotes of an interviewed subject's speech? Is the subject of an interview always a reliable source?

5. What type of story is "Civil Rights; King Sees a Dual Mission" (on page 133)? Can you identify another article in this collection that is the same type of story? What elements helped you come to your conclusion?

6. What is the intention of the article "The Lone Journalist on the Scene When King Was Shot and the Newsroom He Rallied" (on page 167)? How effectively does the piece achieve its purpose?

7. The article "Tongue-Tied Justice" (on page 207) is an example of an op-ed. Identify how the attitude, tone and perspective of The New York Times's editorial board help convey its opinion on the topic.

Citations

All citations in this list are formatted according to the Modern Language Association's (MLA) style guide.

BOOK CITATION

THE NEW YORK TIMES EDITORIAL STAFF. *Martin Luther King Jr.* New York: New York Times Educational Publishing, 2019.

ARTICLE CITATIONS

BARRETT, GEORGE. "Bus Integration in Alabama Calm." *The New York Times*, 22 Dec. 1956, timesmachine.nytimes.com/timesmachine/1956/12/22/84717763.html.

BARRETT, GEORGE. "Shot Hits Home Of Bus Bias Foe." *The New York Times*, 24 Dec. 1956, timesmachine.nytimes.com/timesmahine/1956/12/24/84946443.html.

CALDWELL, EARL. "Court Bars March in Memphis; Dr. King Calls Order 'Illegal.' " *The New York Times*, 4 Apr. 1968, timesmachine.nytimes.com/timesmachine/1968/04/04/88934419.html.

CURRIVAN, GENE. "Dr. King Urges Nonviolence in Rights Protests." *The New York Times*, 15 Mar. 1964, www.nytimes.com/1964/03/15/dr-king-urges-non-violence-in-rights-protests.html.

DAVIES, LAWRENCE E. "Dr. King's Response." *The New York Times*, 13 Apr. 1967, timesmachine.nytimes.com/timesmachine/1967/04/13/90323550.html.

FRANKLIN, BEN A. "Dr. King Plans Mass Protest in Capital June 15." *The New York Times*, 30 Mar. 1968, timesmachine.nytimes.com/timesmachine/1968/03/20/77094903.html.

FRANKLIN, BEN A. "Dr. King to Start March on the Capital April 22." *The New York Times*, 5 Mar. 1968, timesmachine.nytimes.com/timesmachine/1968/03/05/89323131.html.

HERBERS, JOHN. "Civil Rights and War." *The New York Times*, 5 July 1965, www.nytimes.com/1965/07/05/archives/civil-rights-and-war-peace-movements-and-negro-groups-seen-as.html.

HERBERS, JOHN. "67 Negroes Jailed in Alabama Drive." *The New York Times*, 20 Jan. 1965, www.nytimes.com/1965/01/20/archives/67-negroes-jailed-in-alabama-drive-dr-king-seeks-injunction-against.html.

HILL, GLADWIN. "Dr. King Advocates Quitting Vietnam." *The New York Times*, 26 Feb. 1967, timesmachine.nytimes.com/timesmachine/1967/02/26/90272477.html.

HOFMANN, PAUL. "Dr. King Is Backed for Peace Ticket." *The New York Times*, 22 Apr. 1967, timesmachine.nytimes.com/timesmachine/1967/04/22/90338955.html.

INTERNATIONAL HERALD TRIBUNE. "Dr. King, 300 Negroes Arrested in Selma." *The New York Times*, 1 Feb. 2015, iht-retrospective.blogs.nytimes.com/2015/02/01/1965-dr-king-300-negroes-arrested-in-selma/.

INTERNATIONAL HERALD TRIBUNE. "Martin Luther King Jr. Awarded Nobel Peace Prize." *The New York Times*, 14 Oct. 2014, iht-retrospective.blogs.nytimes.com/2014/10/14/1964-martin-luther-king-jr-awarded-nobel-peace-prize/.

JACKSON, JESSE. "How Dr. King Lived Is Why He Died." *The New York Times*, 3 Apr. 2018, www.nytimes.com/2018/04/03/opinion/jesse-jackson-martin-luther-king.html.

LOFTUS, JOSEPH A. "Negro Leaders Confer With President and Rogers at White House." *The New York Times*, 24 June 1958, timesmachine.nytimes.com/timesmachine/1958/06/24/89102380.html.

MARGOLICK, DAVID. "The Lone Journalist on the Scene When King Was Shot and the Newsroom He Rallied." *The New York Times*, 3 Apr. 2018, www.nytimes.com/2018/04/03/insider/the-lone-journalist-on-the-scene-when-king-was-shot-and-the-newsroom-he-rallied.html.

THE NEW YORK TIMES. "Battle Against Tradition: Martin Luther King Jr." *The New York Times*, 21 Mar. 1956, timesmachine.nytimes.com/timesmachine/1956/03/21/84878577.html.

THE NEW YORK TIMES. "Dr. King Is Jailed in a Traffic Case." *The New York Times*, 26 Oct. 1960, timesmachine.nytimes.com/timesmachine/1960/10/26/99815178.html.

THE NEW YORK TIMES. "Dr. King, Negro Leader, Stabbed By Woman in a Store in Harlem." *The New York Times*, 21 Sept. 1958, timesmachine.nytimes.com/timesmachine/1958/09/21/91407398.html.

THE NEW YORK TIMES. "Dr. King's Error." *The New York Times*, 7 Apr. 1967, timesmachine.nytimes.com/timesmachine/1967/04/07/90316200.html.

THE NEW YORK TIMES. "Dr. King Stricken with Pneumonia." *The New York Times*, 23 Sept. 1958, timesmachine.nytimes.com/timesmachine/1958/09/23/91409455.html.

THE NEW YORK TIMES. "Dr. King to Train 3,000 as Leaders For Capital March." *The New York Times*, 17 Jan. 1968, timesmachine.nytimes.com/timesmachine/1968/01/17/88922240.html.

THE NEW YORK TIMES. "Dr. King to Weigh Civil Disobedience If War Intensifies." *The New York Times*, 2 Apr. 1967, timesmachine.nytimes.com/timesmachine/1967/04/02/83043950.html.

THE NEW YORK TIMES. "Dr. King Will Join A Vietnam Protest On April 15 at U.N." *The New York Times*, 17 Mar. 1967, timesmachine.nytimes.com/timesmachine/1967/03/17/83035446.html.

THE NEW YORK TIMES. "14 Negroes Jailed in Atlanta Sit-Ins." *The New York Times*, 20 Oct. 1960, timesmachine.nytimes.com/timesmachine/1960/10/20/99885689.html.

THE NEW YORK TIMES. "Guard Called Out; Curfew Is Ordered in Memphis, but Fires and Looting Erupt." *The New York Times*, 5 Apr. 1968, timesmachine.nytimes.com/timesmachine/1968/04/05/90666174.html.

THE NEW YORK TIMES. "Leaders at Rites; High and Lowly Join in Last Tribute to Rights Champion." *The New York Times*, 9 Apr. 1968, timesmachine.nytimes.com/timesmachine/1968/04/10/89130643.html.

THE NEW YORK TIMES. "N.A.A.C.P. Decries Stand Of Dr. King on Vietnam." *The New York Times*, 11 Apr. 1967, timesmachine.nytimes.com/timesmachine/1967/04/11/83586963.html.

THE NEW YORK TIMES. "President's Plea." *The New York Times*, 5 Apr. 1968, timesmachine.nytimes.com/timesmachine/1968/04/05/90666175.html.

THE NEW YORK TIMES. "Tongue-Tied Justice." *The New York Times*, 11 Mar. 1969, timesmachine.nytimes.com/timesmachine/1969/03/11/90063827.html.

THE NEW YORK TIMES. "The Voice of Negro Leadership." *The New York Times*, 27 July 1967, timesmachine.nytimes.com/timesmachine/1967/07/27/83624073.html.

THE NEW YORK TIMES. "Widespread Disorders; Racial Clashes in Several Cities." *The New York Times*, 5 Apr. 1968, timesmachine.nytimes.com/timesmachine/1968/04/05/90666185.html.

PHILLIPS, WAYNE. "Negro Minister Convicted Of Directing Bus Boycott." *The New York Times*, 23 Mar. 1956, www.nytimes.com/1956/03/23/archives/negro-minister-convicted-of-directing-bus-boycott-negro-minister-is.html.

PHILLIPS, WAYNE. "Negroes Pledge to Keep Boycott." *The New York Times*, 24 Feb. 1956, timesmachine.nytimes.com/timesmachine/1956/02/24/313808222.html.

REED, ROY. "Freedom March Begins at Selma." *The New York Times*, 22 Mar. 1965, www.nytimes.com/1965/03/22/archives/freedom-march-begins-at-selma-troops-on-guard-3200-take-part-in.html.

RESTON, JAMES. " 'I Have a Dream ...' " *The New York Times*, 29 Aug. 1963, timesmachine.nytimes.com/timesmachine/1963/08/29/89957613.html.

ROBERTS, GENE. "Civil Rights; King Sees a Dual Mission." *The New York Times*, 7 May 1967, timesmachine.nytimes.com/timesmachine/1967/05/07/83597095.html.

ROBERTS, GENE. "Dr. King and the War." *The New York Times*, 14 Apr. 1967, timesmachine.nytimes.com/timesmachine/1967/04/14/86714766.html.

ROBERTS, GENE. "Dr. King Stresses Pride in His Race." *The New York Times*, 19 Aug. 1967, timesmachine.nytimes.com/timesmachine/1967/08/19/90394221.html.

ROBERTS, GENE. "Mass Integration Is Quiet in South." *The New York Times*, 31 Aug. 1965, timesmachine.nytimes.com/timesmachine/1965/08/31/101566195.html.

ROBINSON, DOUGLAS. "Dr. King Proposes a Boycott of War." *The New York Times*, 5 Apr. 1967, timesmachine.nytimes.com/timesmachine/1967/04/05/90311327.html.

ROBINSON, DOUGLAS. "King Warns Cities of Summer Riots." *The New York Times*, 17 Apr. 1967, timesmachine.nytimes.com/timesmachine/1967/04/17/90334081.html.

ROBINSON, DOUGLAS. "100,000 Rally at U.N. Against Vietnam War." *The New York Times*, 16 Apr. 1967, timesmachine.nytimes.com/timesmachine/1967/04/16/90327001.html.

ROWLAND, STANLEY. "2,500 Here Hail Boycott Leader." *The New York Times*, 26 Mar. 1956, www.nytimes.com/1956/03/26/archives/2500-here-hail-boycott-leader-head-of-montgomery-negro-bus-protest.html.

RUGABER, WALTER. "Civil Rights; Strong Challenge by King." *The New York Times*, 11 Feb. 1968, timesmachine.nytimes.com/timesmachine/1968/02/11/91220821.html.

RUGABER, WALTER. "Dr. King Declines Peace Candidacy." *The New York Times*, 26 Apr. 1967, timesmachine.nytimes.com/timesmachine/1967/04/26/129255772.html.

RUGABER, WALTER. "Dr. King Planning To Disrupt Capital In Drive for Jobs." *The New York Times*, 5 Dec. 1967, timesmachine.nytimes.com/timesmachine/1967/12/05/82163899.html.

RUGABER, WALTER. "A Negro Is Killed in Memphis March." *The New York Times*, 29 Mar. 1968, timesmachine.nytimes.com/timesmachine/1968/03/29/88932947.html.

RUGABER, WALTER. "Plea by Mrs. King: 'Fulfill His Dream.' " *The New York Times*, 7 Apr. 1968, www.nytimes.com/1968/04/07/archives/plea-by-mrs-king-fulfill-his-dream-plea-by-mrs-king-fulfill-his.html.

SCHUMACH, MURRAY. "Martin Luther King Jr.: Leader of Millions in Nonviolent Drive for Racial Justice." *The New York Times*, 5 Apr. 1968, timesmachine.nytimes.com/timesmachine/1968/04/05/90666312.html.

SITTON, CLAUDE. "Birmingham Jails 1,000 More Negroes." *The New York Times*, 7 May 1963, www.nytimes.com/1963/05/07/archives/birmingham-jails-1000-more-negroes-waves-of-chanting-students.html.

SITTON, CLAUDE."Dr. King Favors Buyers' Boycott." *The New York Times*, 16 Apr. 1960, timesmachine.nytimes.com/timesmachine/1960/04/16/105427506.html.

SITTON, CLAUDE. "Dr. King, Symbol Of the Segregation Struggle." *The New York Times*, 22 Jan. 1961, www.nytimes.com/1961/01/22/archives/dr-king-symbol-of-the-segregation-struggle-symbol-of-segregation.html.

SITTON, CLAUDE. "Negro Sitdowns Stir Fear Of Wider Unrest in South." *The New York Times*, 15 Feb. 1960, www.nytimes.com/1960/02/15/archives/negro-sitdowns-stir-fear-of-wider-unrest-in-south-negro-sitdowns.html.

SMITH, HENDRICK. "Dr. King's 3 Children Visit Him; He Is Allowed Out of Jail Cell." *The New York Times*, 6 Aug. 1962, timesmachine.nytimes.com/timesmachine/1962/08/06/90174045.html.

VAN GELDER, LAWRENCE. "Dismay in Nation; Negroes Urge Others to Carry on Spirit of Nonviolence." *The New York Times*, 5 Apr. 1968, timesmachine.nytimes.com/timesmachine/1968/04/05/90666182.html.

WAGGONER, WALTER H. "Shift in Position Is Hinted By King; He Says He May Be Forced to Pick a Candidate." *The New York Times*, 28 Mar. 1968, timesmachine.nytimes.com/timesmachine/1968/03/28/77082151.html.

WALZ, JAY. "Negroes Hold Rally On Rights in Capital." *The New York Times*, 18 May 1957, timesmachine.nytimes.com/timesmachine/1957/05/18/121569692.html.

Index